CONFERENCE PROCEEDINGS

PROTECTING EMERGENCY RESPONDERS

LESSONS LEARNED FROM TERRORIST ATTACKS

Brian A. Jackson, D. J. Peterson, James T. Bartis, Tom LaTourrette, Irene Brahmakulam, Ari Houser, Jerry Sollinger

Supported by the
Office of Science and Technology Policy

RAND
SCIENCE AND TECHNOLOGY POLICY INSTITUTE

The research described in this report was conducted by RAND's Science and Technology Policy Institute, under Contract ENG-9812731.

ISBN: 0-8330-3149-X

Cover photo from Reuters/TimePix.
Peter Morgan, photographer. Reproduced with permission.

Cover design by Maritta Tapanainen

Published 2002 by RAND
1700 Main Street, P.O. Box 2138, Santa Monica, CA 90407-2138
1200 South Hayes Street, Arlington, VA 22202-5050
201 North Craig Street, Suite 202, Pittsburgh, PA 15213
RAND URL: http://www.rand.org/
To order RAND documents or to obtain additional information, contact Distribution Services: Telephone: (310) 451-7002;
Fax: (310) 451-6915; Email: order@rand.org

PREFACE

On December 9–11, 2001, a conference was held in New York City that brought together individuals with experience in responding to acts of terrorism. The purpose of the conference was to hear and document the firsthand experiences of emergency responders regarding the performance, availability, and appropriateness of their personal protective equipment as they responded to these incidents. The meeting considered the responses to the September 11, 2001, attacks at the World Trade Center and the Pentagon; the 1995 attack at the Alfred P. Murrah Federal Building in Oklahoma City, Oklahoma; and the emergency responses to the anthrax incidents that occurred in several locations through autumn 2001. The conference was sponsored by the National Institute for Occupational Safety and Health of the U.S. Centers for Disease Control and Prevention, which also arranged for RAND to organize and conduct the conference and prepare this report.

This report presents a synthesis of the discussions held at the December meeting. It is intended to help federal managers and decisionmakers

- Understand the unique working and safety environment associated with terrorist incidents.
- Develop a comprehensive personal protective technology research agenda.
- Improve federal education and training programs and activities directed at the health and safety of emergency responders.

The report should also help state and municipal officials, trade union leaders, industry executives, and researchers obtain a better understanding of equipment and training needs for protecting emergency workers.

This conference report builds on previous RAND studies, including

- William Schwabe, Lois M. Davis, and Brian A. Jackson, *Challenges and Choices for Crime-Fighting Technology: Federal Support of State and Local*

Law Enforcement, MR-1349-OSTP/NIJ, RAND, Santa Monica, California, 2001, available at http://www.rand.org/publications/MR/MR1349/.

- Mark A. Schuster et al., "A National Survey of Stress Reactions After the September 11, 2001 Terrorist Attacks," *New England Journal of Medicine,* 345:1507–1511, 2001.
- DJ Peterson, Tom LaTourrette, and James T. Bartis, *New Forces at Work in Mining: Industry Views of Critical Technologies,* MR-1324-OSTP, RAND, Santa Monica, California, 2001, available at http://www.rand.org/publications/MR/MR1324/.
- Ronald D. Fricker, Jr. et al., *Pesticide Use During the Gulf War: A Survey of Gulf War Veterans,* MR-1018/12-OSD, RAND, Santa Monica, California, 2000, available at http://www.rand.org/publications/MR/MR1018.12/.

THE SCIENCE AND TECHNOLOGY POLICY INSTITUTE

Originally created by Congress in 1991 as the Critical Technologies Institute and renamed in 1998, the Science and Technology Policy Institute is a federally funded research and development center sponsored by the National Science Foundation and managed by RAND. The Institute's mission is to help improve public policy by conducting objective, independent research and analysis on policy issues that involve science and technology. To this end, the Institute

- Supports the Office of Science and Technology Policy and other Executive Branch agencies, offices, and councils.
- Helps science and technology decisionmakers understand the likely consequences of their decisions and choose among alternative policies.
- Helps improve understanding in both the public and private sectors of the ways in which science and technology can better serve national objectives.

In carrying out its mission, the Institute consults broadly with representatives from private industry, institutions of higher education, and other nonprofit institutions.

Inquiries regarding the Science and Technology Policy Institute may be directed to the address below.

Dr. Helga Rippen
Director, RAND Science and Technology Policy Institute
1200 South Hayes Street
Arlington, VA 22202-5050
Phone: (703) 413-1100 x5574
Web: http://www.rand.org/scitech/stpi/
Email: stpi@rand.org

CONTENTS

Appendix

EXECUTIVE SUMMARY

Just as it has for the nation as a whole, the world in which emergency responders work has changed in fundamental ways since September 11, 2001. Members of professions already defined by their high levels of risk now face new, often unknown threats on the job. At a basic level, the September 11 terrorist events have forced emergency responders to see the incidents they are asked to respond to in a new light. At the World Trade Center, 450 emergency responders perished while responding to the terrorist attacks—about one-sixth of the total number of victims. Hundreds more were seriously injured. In this light, the terrorist events are also forcing emergency responders to reconsider the equipment and practices they use to protect themselves in the line of duty.

Preparation is key to protecting the health and safety of emergency responders, and valuable lessons can be learned from previous responses. To this end, the National Institute for Occupational Safety and Health (NIOSH) sponsored and asked the RAND Science and Technology Policy Institute to organize a conference of individuals with firsthand knowledge of emergency response to terrorist attacks. The purpose of the conference was to review the adequacy of personal protective equipment (PPE) and practices, such as training, and to make recommendations on how the equipment and practices worked and how they might be improved. Attendees included persons who responded to the 1995 attack on the Alfred P. Murrah Federal Building in Oklahoma City, the September 11 attacks on the World Trade Center and the Pentagon, and the anthrax incidents that occurred during autumn 2001. They represented a wide range of occupations and skills: firefighters, police, emergency medical technicians, construction workers, union officials, and government representatives from local, state, and federal agencies. The conference was held December 9–11, 2001, in New York City, and this report synthesizes the discussions that took place there.

NEW RISKS, NEW ROLES FOR EMERGENCY RESPONDERS

Although the terrorist incidents shared some characteristics with large natural disasters, the NIOSH/RAND conference participants highlighted ways in which those incidents posed unique challenges. They were large in scale, long in duration, and complex in terms of the range of hazards presented. As a result of these characteristics, these events thrust responders into new roles for which they may not have been properly prepared or equipped. The themes of scale, duration, and range of hazards were repeated frequently during the discussions at the conference because they were seen as having critical implications for protecting the health and safety of emergency responders—during both the immediate, urgent phase and the sustained campaign phase of the responses.

The September 11 terrorist incidents were notable for their large scale—in terms of both the damage incurred and the human and material resources needed to respond. Conference participants spoke extensively about the difficulty of conducting search and rescue, fire suppression, and shoring and stabilization operations, as well as hazard monitoring. Responses were hampered by collateral developments, in particular the grounding of commercial air transport, which slowed the implementation of command and logistical support infrastructures.

The responses to the terrorist attacks involved days and weeks of constant work. At the World Trade Center, an initial urgent phase persisted for several days and then gradually transitioned into a sustained campaign that lasted for several months. An important message of the conference was that PPE generally worked well for its designed purpose in the initial response. However, such equipment typically was not designed for the continuous use associated with a sustained response campaign. Firefighter turnout gear, for example, is constructed to be worn for, at most, hours. Accordingly, responders spoke of being hampered by basic problems such as wet garments and blistered feet.

Furthermore, at major terrorist-attack sites, emergency workers face a staggering range of hazards. Not only do they confront the usual hazards associated with building fires—flames, heat, combustion by-products, smoke—they also must be prepared to deal with rubble and debris, air choked with fine particles, human remains, hazardous materials (anhydrous ammonia, freon, battery acids), and the potential risk of secondary devices or a follow-on attack. Conference participants indicated that many currently available PPE ensembles and training practices were not designed to protect responders from this range of hazards or were not supplied in sufficient quantity at the attack sites to meet the scale of the problem.

The scale of the terrorist events, their duration, and the range of hazards required that many emergency responders take on atypical tasks for which they were insufficiently equipped and trained. The nature of the destruction at the World Trade Center and the Pentagon reduced opportunities for primary reconnaissance and rescue—important tasks for firefighters in large structural fires. Conversely, firefighters became engaged in activities they usually do not do: "busting up and hauling concrete," scrambling over a rubble pile, and removing victims and decayed bodies and body parts.

Construction workers were also deployed at the scenes and placed in hazardous environments early on. In all of the terrorist-incident responses, emergency medical personnel were on-scene, performing rescue operations, for example, in the rubble pile at the World Trade Center. Complicating activity at these already chaotic, hazardous, and demanding attack sites was the fact that the sites are also crime scenes. In addition, there were massive influxes of skilled and unskilled volunteers that created a significant challenge in managing the incident sites and assuring that all were properly protected.

In sum, the definition and roles of an *emergency responder* expanded greatly in the wake of the terrorist attacks, but few of the responders had adequate PPE, training, or information for such circumstances.

PERSONAL PROTECTIVE EQUIPMENT PERFORMANCE AND AVAILABILITY

From the experiences at these attack sites, it is clear that there were significant shortfalls in the way responders were protected. Many responders suggested that the PPE even impeded their ability to accomplish their missions.

Within the overall PPE ensemble used by responders at these sites, some equipment performed better than others. While head protection and high-visibility vests functioned relatively well for most responders, protective clothing and respirators exhibited serious shortcomings. Conference participants reported that the available garments did not provide sufficient protection against biological and infectious disease hazards, the heat of fires at the sites, and the demanding physical environment of unstable rubble piles, nor were they light and flexible enough to allow workers to move debris and enter confined spaces. Attendees also indicated that the available eye protection, while protecting well against direct impact injury, provided almost no protection against the persistent dust at the World Trade Center site.

Of all personal protective equipment, respiratory protection elicited the most extended discussion across all of the professional panels. Attendees indicated that under most circumstances, the self-contained breathing apparatus (SCBA) was grossly limited by both the weight of the systems and the short lengths of time (about 15 to 30 minutes) they can be used before their air bottles must be refilled. Most participants complained that respirators reduced their field of vision at best, and their facepieces fogged up at worst. Filters for air-purifying respirators (APRs) often did not match available facepieces, and many responders questioned the level of protection they provided, especially during anthrax responses.

For almost all protective technologies, responders indicated serious problems with equipment not being comfortable enough to allow extended wear during demanding physical labor. It was frequently observed that current technologies require a tradeoff between the amount of protection they provide and the extent to which they are light enough, practical enough, and wearable enough to allow responders to do their jobs. While conference attendees were concerned about having adequate protection, many were even more concerned about equipment hindering them from accomplishing their rescue and recovery missions in an arduous and sustained campaign. Respirators available at the sites were uncomfortable, causing many wearers to use them only intermittently (one participant dubbed them "neck protectors") or to discard them after a short period.

For many firefighters at the conference, PPE availability was as important a concern as PPE performance. Some health-and-safety panelists expressed a similar view. There was an acute shortage of respirators early in the response at the World Trade Center, for example. Subsequently, providing appropriate equipment to the large numbers of workers at these sites was made even more difficult because of the many types and brands of equipment that were being used by the various responder organizations or were being supplied from various sources. The problem was further exacerbated by a lack of interoperability among different types of equipment. These issues, coupled with the very large volume of equipment sent to the World Trade Center site, in particular, made it very difficult to match responders with appropriate equipment and supplies.

PERSONAL PROTECTIVE EQUIPMENT TRAINING AND INFORMATION

The responses to the terrorist attacks uncovered a range of PPE training and information needs. Before an incident occurs, those who are likely to be involved in a response should be trained on the proper selection and operation of personal protective equipment. Emergency medical technicians who were themselves treating casualties in the heart of the disaster site should have been wearing PPE but frequently were not, in large part because this equipment was not part of their standard training regimen.

The experiences in these incidents also showed that there is a need for significant on-site training to protect the health and safety of workers. The attack sites involved large numbers of workers, particularly construction workers and volunteers, many of whom were not familiar with most PPE. They needed to be trained in the proper selection and fitting of respirators, how to maintain them, and when to change filters. The situation with anthrax was more severe. Health and safety panel members felt that training support during the anthrax attacks was inadequate on all fronts: The response protocols were being developed *during* the actual responses.

Emergency responders repeatedly stressed the importance of having timely and reliable health and safety information. "What kills rescue responders is the unknown," commented an emergency medical services (EMS) panel member. Several shortcomings were noted by conference participants. Special-operations and law-enforcement responders reported problems caused by different information sources telling them different things. Such information conflicts were often attributed to differences in risk assessment and PPE standards among reporting parties. Especially in the case of the anthrax incidents, keeping up with changing information being provided by numerous agencies was a serious challenge for front-line responder organizations. For many conference participants, the problem was not a lack of information on hazards. Rather, they spoke of difficulties trying to manage and make sense of a surplus of information. Finally, conference attendees suggested that better and more consistent information provision could motivate responders to wear PPE and could decrease the tendency to modify it or take it off when it becomes uncomfortable.

SITE MANAGEMENT

One message that emerged clearly from virtually all panel discussions is that proper site management had a decisive effect on whether personal protective equipment was available, appropriately prescribed, used, and maintained.

The most critical need for site management is a coherent command authority. An effective command structure is essential to begin solving three critical issues affecting PPE: information provision, equipment logistics, and enforcement. Due to logistical problems early in the response, for example, supplies of PPE were misplaced, the stocks of equipment that were available were largely unknown, and responders often did not receive or could not find the equipment they needed.

Conference attendees also emphasized the need for immediate and effective perimeter or scene control. Initially, this entailed responders personally "holding people back" and isolating the scene. As the response evolved, it was necessary to erect a "hard perimeter," such as a chain-link fence, to make sure only essential personnel operating under the direction of the scene commander were on-site.

Conference attendees also indicated that enforcement of PPE use is very important. Although panelists acknowledged that there is a period early in a chaotic response when it is not practical to rigorously enforce the use of protective equipment, they indicated that strict enforcement must eventually begin in order to protect the health of the responders. Other factors that complicated enforcement of PPE use were the large number of organizations (with different PPE standards) operating on-site, the lack of a unified command, and shortcomings in scene control. Because of the difficulty of defining when it is appropriate to begin enforcing PPE use—and removing workers from the site if they do not comply with use requirements—attendees indicated that this role might be best played by an organization not directly involved in or affected by the incident.

RECOMMENDATIONS

After having discussed PPE performance, information and training, and site-management issues, NIOSH/RAND conference participants were asked to put forward concrete recommendations about technologies and procedures that could help protect the health and safety of emergency workers as they respond to acts of terrorism. The following points represent a brief sample of the themes that emerged and the solutions put forth by conference discussants.

Personal Protective Equipment Performance

- Develop guidelines for the appropriate PPE ensembles for long-duration disaster responses involving rubble, human remains, and a range of respiratory threats. If appropriate equipment is not currently available, address any roadblocks to its development. Such equipment could be applicable to other major disasters, such as earthquakes or tornadoes, as well as to terrorist attacks.
- Define the appropriate ensembles of PPE needed to safely and efficiently respond to biological incidents, threats, and false alarms. Key considerations include providing comparable levels of protection for all responders and addressing the logistical and decontamination issues associated with large numbers of responses in short time periods.

Personal Protective Equipment Availability

- Explore mechanisms to effectively outfit all responders at large incident sites with appropriate personal protective equipment as rapidly as possible.
- Examine any barriers to equipment standardization or interoperability among emergency-responder organizations. Strategies could include coordination of equipment procurement among organizations or work with equipment manufacturers to promote broader interoperability within classes of equipment.

Training and Information

- Define mechanisms to rapidly and effectively provide responders at incident sites with useful information about the hazards they face and the equipment they need for protection. Approaches could include more-effective coordination among relevant organizations and development of technologies that provide responders with individual, real-time information about their environment.
- Explore ways to ensure that responders at large-scale disaster sites are appropriately trained to use the protective equipment they are provided. All types of responders must be addressed, and mechanisms that provide training and experience with the equipment before a disaster occurs should be investigated.
- Consider logistical requirements of extended response activities during disaster drills and training. Such activities provide response commanders with information on the logistical constraints that could restrict response capabilities.

Management

- Provide guidelines and define organizational responsibilities for enforcing protective-equipment use at major disaster sites. While such guidelines must address the risks responders are willing to take when the potential exists to save lives, they must also consider that during long-term responses, the health and safety of responders should be a principal concern.
- Develop mechanisms to allow rapid and efficient scene control at disaster sites as early as possible during a response.

ACKNOWLEDGMENTS

NIOSH and RAND wish to thank all of the emergency responders, public health professionals, and federal, state, and local workers who participated in the workshops for their time, candor, and good will.

The support, guidance, and assistance of representatives of the Organizing Partners of the conference enabled NIOSH and RAND to bring together a broadly experienced group of emergency responders. Assistance from Jim Gass of the Oklahoma City National Memorial Institute for the Prevention of Terrorism made possible the participation of individuals who responded to the attack on the Murrah Federal Office Building. Kathleen Higgins and Philip Mattson of the National Institute of Standards and Technology Office of Law Enforcement Standards provided important assistance in establishing the law-enforcement panel. Paul Bergeron coordinated support from the U.S. Department of Defense and the InterAgency Board for Equipment Standardization and Inter-Operability, as did Stephen Foley and Gary Tokle for the National Fire Protection Association, and Carl E. Hildebrand for the White House Office of Science and Technology Policy.

For extensive assistance and insights in developing this conference, we extend special thanks to David Prezant, Deputy Chief Medical Officer of the Fire Department of New York, Dean Cox of the Fairfax County (Virginia) Fire and Rescue Department, and Bill Haskell of the U.S. Army Soldier and Biological Chemical Command.

The conference would not have been possible without the support of the International Association of Fire Fighters (IAFF) and the International Association of Fire Chiefs (IAFC). We are especially grateful for the assistance and guidance provided by Andy Levinson of the IAFF in developing the conference and facilitating the attendance of rank-and-file emergency workers with direct experience in responding to terrorist attacks.

We also thank our RAND colleagues David Adamson and Scott Hassell, who assisted us during the conference and also contributed to this report.

At NIOSH, Richard Metzler and H. Kenneth Sacks guided RAND's organization and management of the conference, and we thank them for their enthusiasm and support, which were critical to keeping the conference and this report on a fast track. Andrea Okun, Marie Haring-Sweeney, Ralph Zumwalde, and Carol Merry Stephenson took on the task of selecting, funding, and managing the firm of Kerback and Company, Inc., which provided facilitators for the panel sessions.

Special thanks are due to the International Safety Equipment Association (ISEA) and, in particular, its President, Daniel Shipp, and its Technical Director, Janice Bradley. Beyond organizational assistance, ISEA graciously hosted a night-before-the-conference reception.

While the content of this report reflects the observations and opinions of the participants in the conference, the authors accept the responsibility for the ways those views are expressed in these pages.

ACRONYMS AND ABBREVIATIONS

APR	air-purifying respirator
BDU	battle dress uniform
CDC	U.S. Centers for Disease Control and Prevention
DoD	U.S. Department of Defense
EMS	emergency medical services
EPA	U.S. Environmental Protection Agency
FBI	Federal Bureau of Investigation
FDNY	New York City Fire Department
FEMA	Federal Emergency Management Agency
hazmat	hazardous material
HAZWOPER	Hazardous Waste Operation and Emergency Response stipulated in Federal Regulation 29CFR 1910.120
HEPA	high-efficiency particulate air (filters)
IACP	International Association of Chiefs of Police
IAFC	International Association of Fire Chiefs
IAFF	International Association of Fire Fighters
ID	personal identification
IST	Federal Emergency Management Agency Incident Support Team
MP	Military Police
NIOSH	National Institute for Occupational Safety and Health

NPPTL	National Personal Protective Technology Laboratory
NYPD	New York City Police Department
OSHA	U.S. Occupational Safety and Health Administration
PAPR	powered air-purifying respirator
PASS	personal alert safety system
PD	Police Department
PPE	personal protective equipment
R&D	research and development
SCBA	self-contained breathing apparatus
SWAT	Special Weapons and Tactics
USAR	Urban Search and Rescue
VIP	very important person

Chapter One

INTRODUCTION

Just as it has for the nation as a whole, the world in which emergency responders work has changed in fundamental ways since September 11, 2001. Members of professions already defined by their high levels of risk now face new, often unknown threats on the job. At a basic level, the September 11 terrorist events have forced emergency responders to see the incidents they are asked to respond to in a new light. As one firefighter-special-operations professional put it, "After 9-11, we must rethink exactly how we approach things. If you go to a fire scene and there is a possibility of a terrorist attack, then most of it is unknown. Other than what you see, everything else is unknown."

At the World Trade Center, 450 emergency responders perished in the response to the terrorist attacks—about one-sixth of the total number of victims. Hundreds more were seriously injured. In this light, the terrorist events are also forcing emergency responders to reconsider the equipment and practices they use to protect themselves in the line of duty. A firefighter observed, "We had an incident at the FBI [headquarters] soon after the incident in New York. I was looking at the battalion chief on the scene and watching them operate under a cantilevered structure. I asked them, 'Why don't you move everybody further away so if that thing does come down you won't get killed?' New York taught me a lot about firefighter safety."

Preparation is key to protecting the health and safety of emergency responders, and valuable lessons can be learned from previous responses. To that end, the National Institute for Occupational Safety and Health (NIOSH) convened a conference in New York City on December 9–11, 2001, to determine what could be learned about protecting the life and health of emergency workers who respond to terrorist attacks. The focus was on personal protective equipment (PPE), and the input was provided by workers who responded to the 1995 attack on the Alfred P. Murrah Federal Building in Oklahoma City, Oklahoma; the September 11 attacks on the World Trade Center and the Pentagon; and the anthrax incidents that occurred during autumn 2001. This report summarizes the key lessons learned about PPE during those events.

ABOUT THE CONFERENCE

Purpose

In the wake of the terrorist attacks of 2001, the federal government and the nation are reexamining their ability to respond to acts of terrorism against the United States. As part of this effort, NIOSH and other federal agencies are reviewing lessons learned regarding protecting the life and health of emergency workers who respond to such attacks.

In spring 2001, NIOSH established the National Personal Protective Technology Laboratory (NPPTL). The mission of the NPPTL is to provide leadership in the prevention and reduction of occupational disease, injury, and death for those workers who rely on personal protective technology, through research, partnership, service, and communication. The lessons learned by emergency responders involved in the recent terrorist events and discussed at the conference offer important and timely information that will help in developing the Laboratory's research agenda.

This information will also serve to inform and improve federal education and training programs and activities directed at the occupational health and safety of emergency responders. Because of the broad importance of emergency preparedness and response to the new national priority of homeland defense, the conference information is also expected to interest other audiences at the federal, state, and local level, both inside and outside the emergency-response community.

Organization

NIOSH requested that the RAND Science and Technology Policy Institute organize and lead the conference on its behalf. On November 2, 2001, NIOSH and RAND held an organizational and planning meeting at which representatives of key government and nongovernmental organizations endorsed the December conference and offered their cooperation. Eleven of these organizations elected to be designated as Organizing Partners of the meeting. (The Organizing Partners are listed in Appendix A.) With assistance from the Organizing Partners, NIOSH and RAND were able to attract to the meeting a diverse group of attendees with considerable breadth and depth of experience in responding to terrorist attacks.

The 150 individuals who participated in the NIOSH/RAND conference were selected on the basis of their central roles in responding to these attacks and for their ability to think broadly and creatively about PPE and management issues. Conference participants included both rank-and-file and top-level representatives from local, state, and federal emergency-services organizations; trade unions; health and safety agencies; private-sector equipment and services providers; and government and academic research institutions. Most of the participants had firsthand experience working at the incident sites (many were present on the day of the attacks) or served in a direct support capacity off-site. (The conference participants are listed in Appendix B.)

The conference consisted of a series of plenary sessions followed by breakout discussion groups. (The conference agenda is reproduced in Appendix C. The plenary presentations are summarized in Appendix D.) Participants were assigned to one of eight breakout groups (panels) according to their role in responding to the attacks:

- Firefighters
- Firefighter special operations (2 panels)
- Emergency medical services (EMS)
- Law enforcement
- Construction and other trade services
- Health and safety
- Federal and state agencies

Each panel was guided by a professional facilitator and a specialist knowledgeable about technical issues of concern to the group. A RAND analyst also observed each group. The panels were tasked with addressing a common set of topics, including

- Tasks performed during the initial and sustained phases of the response
- Hazards encountered
- Availability and relevance of personal protective equipment
- Training and information about the use of protective equipment

Participants were free to tailor the discussions to address the issues that were most important to their group's experiences. To encourage candid discussion, the breakout sessions were held on a not-for-attribution basis.

THE REPORT

This report synthesizes the discussions that took place at the conference, many of which included information from individual professionals about response activities that were, in some cases, still ongoing and evolving. This presentation of the conference proceedings seeks to preserve the substance and tenor of the emergency responders' insights. As a result, the statements presented in this report represent the personal views of conference participants at that unique point in time. They do not necessarily represent established or consensus views of the organizations represented or of the greater emergency-responder community.

The conference proceedings are organized as follows: Chapter Two describes the unique characteristics of the sites of major terrorist attacks, concentrating on the perspective of the first responders and the PPE they require. Chapter Three summarizes the key lessons gleaned from the panel discussions with respect to the availability of PPE and how it performed at the attack sites. Chapter Four discusses issues of PPE information dissemination and training. Chapter Five addresses the problems associated with managing a major terrorist attack site, again with a special emphasis on PPE. Chapter Six presents recommendations put forth by the conference participants. The final chapter offers some concluding remarks.

Chapter Two

THE TERRORIST INCIDENTS

The broad outlines of the September 11 attacks, the Oklahoma City bombing, and the autumn 2001 anthrax incidents are well known. In many ways, the events differed greatly. The World Trade Center event was much larger than the others in scale, the amount of damage that occurred, lives lost, and the number of responders involved. Its location in downtown Manhattan made managing the scene very complex. The Pentagon attack occurred at a building whose location facilitated rapid site control. The Murrah Building attack was similar in scale to the Pentagon attack but presented additional difficulties because of its location within an urban area: Adjacent buildings were impacted but not destroyed, and isolating the site was more difficult. The anthrax attacks consisted of a series of biohazard incidents involving cases of real contamination, false alarms, and hoaxes, spread over several months and many jurisdictions nationwide.

Despite their differences, these terrorist incidents and the responses to them share several characteristics that set them apart from most other events requiring emergency response: They were large in scale, long in duration, and presented an array of hazards, many of them unusual. In addition, unlike most other large-scale disaster scenes, the terrorist-attack sites are also crime scenes requiring preservation and collection of evidence for investigation and prosecution. Because of these characteristics, these events thrust responders into new roles for which they may not have been properly prepared or equipped.

The themes of scale, duration, and range of hazards were repeated frequently during the discussions at the conference because they were seen as having critical implications for protecting the health and safety of emergency responders—during both the immediate, urgent phase and the sustained campaign phase of the responses.

OVERVIEW OF THE TERRORIST INCIDENTS

World Trade Center, New York City

At about 8:45 a.m. on September 11, 2001, a hijacked commercial airliner struck the North Tower of the World Trade Center. Shortly after 9:00 a.m., another hijacked aircraft crashed into the South Tower. While evacuation, rescue, and attempted fire-suppression activities were under way, both 110-story towers collapsed, the South Tower at about 10:00 a.m., and the North Tower at about 10:30 a.m. Other buildings in the 16-acre site were seriously damaged, including Building Seven of the World Trade Center complex, which collapsed on the evening of September 11, after an extended blaze. Approximately 3,000 people were killed in the incident, and about 7,000 were injured.

Emergency responders arrived to two high-rise building fires and entered the towers to assist evacuation of the occupants and perform search and rescue and fire-suppression activities. The towers then collapsed, killing hundreds of responders, including the top leadership of the Fire Department of New York City (FDNY) who had been in charge at the scene. A total of 450 responders were killed, including 23 from New York City Police Department, 343 from FDNY, and 74 from the Port Authority of New York and New Jersey. The responders lost in the Trade Towers collapse were among the most experienced, highly trained, and extensively equipped special operations and leadership personnel in their response organizations. Approximately 320 emergency responders were treated for injuries or illnesses at five nearby hospitals; others were treated at temporary triage stations.

Responders and backup supplies were dispatched from all over the country, including 20 Federal Emergency Management Agency (FEMA) Urban Search and Rescue (USAR) task forces. As many as eight USAR teams worked at a time. The last task forces were released on October 7. In January 2002, the New York City government turned over day-to-day management and operation of the site to a private construction company. Debris removal and site stabilization are expected to be completed by December 2002.

Pentagon, Arlington, Virginia

At about 9:40 a.m. on September 11, 2001, a hijacked airliner crashed into the western side of the Pentagon, killing 125 people on the ground, as well as 64 people on board the plane. Area hospitals treated 88 injured people. The crash damaged or destroyed three of the five interior concentric "rings" of the Pentagon building. The section where the plane hit had been recently renovated, and many offices were empty or being used for storage at the time.

Local responders arrived immediately, and other agencies, including five USAR teams, came to assist. The Arlington County Fire Department set up an incident command system and coordinated the emergency response. The rescue and recovery phase lasted 11 days, after which Arlington County transferred responsibility for the incident and site management to the Federal Bureau of Investigation (FBI), on September 21. No responders were killed. Demolition of the damaged area began on October 18 and was completed on November 29. Reconstruction of the damaged area is expected to be completed in Spring 2003.

Murrah Federal Building, Oklahoma City

Just after 9 a.m. on April 19, 1995, a truck bomb exploded in front of the Alfred P. Murrah Federal Building in Oklahoma City. The blast destroyed approximately one-third of the nine-story building and caused damage to several other buildings in the area. The blast killed a total of 167 people and injured more than 600.

The Oklahoma City Fire Department responded immediately, set up an incident command structure, and was in charge of the search and rescue operations. The FBI was in charge of the criminal investigation. Many organizations were involved in the response, including 11 USAR task forces from around the country. Search and rescue operations continued for 17 days. A volunteer responder was killed by falling debris, bringing the total number of deaths to 168. The building was demolished on May 23, 1995.

Anthrax Incidents

Between early October and early December 2001, five people died from anthrax infection, and at least 13 others contracted the disease in Washington, D.C.; New York City; Trenton, New Jersey; and Boca Raton, Florida. Anthrax spores were found in a number of government buildings and postal facilities in these and other areas. Most of the confirmed anthrax cases were tied to contaminated letters mailed to media personalities and U.S. Senators. Thousands of people were potentially exposed to the spores and took preventive antibiotics. Numerous mail facilities and government buildings were shut down for investigation and decontamination.

In the wake of these incidents, federal, state, and local emergency-response agencies across the United States had to respond to thousands of calls to investigate suspicious packages, unknown powders, and other suspected exposures. Almost all of these incidents turned out not to involve an actual biohazard. Nevertheless, emergency responders typically treated each call as entailing a serious health and safety risk.

LONG-TERM CAMPAIGNS

Conventional emergency situations, such as building fires, typically require responders to face risks for discrete and short periods of time, usually measured in minutes or hours. Most PPE and operating procedures are designed for such situations. In contrast, the responses to the terrorist attacks involved days and weeks of constant work. At the World Trade Center, an initial urgent phase persisted for several days and then gradually transitioned into a sustained campaign that lasted for several months.

For those who had it, structural firefighting gear—including helmet, self-contained breathing apparatus (SCBA) or air pack, and turnout gear (thermally insulated coat, pants, and boots)—worked well for short periods, especially during the initial responses. However, this equipment is not suitable for a sustained campaign. Fire service helmets are heavy and can hinder performance. In addition to SCBA being heavy and cumbersome, the facepieces fog, reducing

> One of the differences here, as we talk about terrorist events, is, this is not your average fire. There's no [fire] getting knocked down in 15 to 20 minutes, go take rehab . . . and go home. These are long-term events, and first-alarm units, at least with us, were on the scene for hours, taking the gear off, rehabbing somewhere in the general area where they were working, finding another [air] bottle somewhere and refilling it. . . . In terrorist-type events, they're going to be campaign, long-term incidents where people are going to be using this gear and putting it back on wet, half-used bottles—going through a lot of things that we would not consider the norm.
>
> —*Firefighter-special-operations panel member*

visibility, and the equipment hinders verbal and radio communication. The air pack makes it difficult to fit into confined spaces. With limited air in each tank, bottles at the attack sites had to be switched, but many organizations lacked sufficient on-site refill capacity. In many cases, responders reported that air-purifying respirator (APR) filter cartridges were used far longer than they were designed to be used, resulting in filters becoming clogged and the respirators being rendered ineffective. Many respirators were uncomfortable, causing "mask face," which motivated many workers to discard them after short periods or use a lighter dust mask instead. Some cut slits in their masks to facilitate smoking. "To cut right to the chase," stated one firefighter, "the equipment that we have isn't comfortable or practical for a long duration."

> I never put my bunker gear on from day one. Most I ever had was my bunker coat and my helmet, because I knew that if I walked around in that debris for one to two hours, my feet were done in bunker boots.
>
> —*Firefighter-special-operations panel member*

Turnout gear is heavy and hot, and many responders suffered from fatigue and heat exhaustion. Contact lenses tended to dry out when worn with respirators for long periods. Wet shoes and socks caused blisters.[1] Trades panel members believed that many more workers than were reported had blisters but simply self-medicated or tried to ignore them. Because of the discomfort, responders would take off their gear whenever they believed they could do so without causing immediate harm, leaving them with no protection at all.

Following the announcement of the first case of anthrax exposure in early October 2001, law-enforcement and other emergency responders had to follow

---

[1]A panelist pointed to an unpublished report, the *World Trade Center Worker Injury and Illness Surveillance Update*, New York City Department of Health, November 20, 2001, which indicated that 440 people working at the World Trade Center site sought treatment for blisters. The report covered injuries and illnesses from September 14 to November 18, 2001.

> After a while, sometimes, I guess, you develop this cavalier attitude and you think, "Here we go, another call, another white powdery substance." It's probably all b.s., but you still have to go. The way we treat something may not be the way the hazmat team treats it, because they're going to treat it a lot more seriously than maybe we will sometimes. And there are times where we feel almost embarrassed to call the hazmat team in, because we know it's probably nothing. But then again, if the post office, if the employees, the union, the manager, everyone is really concerned about it, I'm not going to go out, bleach it, and say, "Okay, it's taken care of," because they're going to say, "What are you, crazy?"
>
> *—Law-enforcement panel member*

up on an avalanche of calls, the vast majority of them false alarms. Postal inspectors alone investigated thousands of cases of possible anthrax in the following months. With the large scale of the response, attitudes toward potential health and safety risks associated with anthrax changed. In many instances, they were relaxed. In the words of one firefighter, "Two years ago, we would have been on the scene for five hours. Now guys are off the scene in five minutes."

LARGE-SCALE EVENTS

The terrorist incidents were noted for their large scale, as epitomized by the twin towers of the World Trade Center (the largest office complex in the world), the Pentagon (the largest office complex under one roof), and the thousands of anthrax scares.

> You're dealing with a work scene that, in the first week or two, had probably two to three thousand, if not more, emergency responders on the scene. Pretty much 24 hours a day. All of them with various backgrounds and training. You had construction workers, you had heavy-equipment operators, you had medical workers, firefighters, police officers, hygienists, military personnel. All of them with different levels of training, different types of equipment. So you had to try and logistically bring in all of the equipment for these people. You're bringing in multiple manufacturers and vendors.
>
> *—Firefighter-special-operations panel member*

Special-operations personnel spoke extensively about the difficulty of conducting search and rescue, fire-suppression, and shoring and stabilization operations at the Pentagon because of the building's massive size and the extent of the damage. Given the scale of the disaster at the World Trade Center, firefighters were forced into a defensive status where they extinguished fires in some adjacent buildings but had to let others burn.

A key component in protecting the health and safety of emergency responders is having the logistical framework necessary to provide them with needed equipment and supplies. Logistical management of the World Trade Center site, particularly in the early days, was overwhelming. The U.S. Environmental Protection Agency (EPA) alone distributed 10,000 respirators at the site in the first few weeks. "We had [flood]lights come in from Iowa. We had $180,000 in six-by-sixes [timbers] delivered in the first four hours," observed an EMS panel member. Another on the panel said, "It was so big geographically, that things were happening remote of you that you had no clue of. The majority of my victims were transported by private automobiles, even though we had an enormous treatment and triage area set up. Enormous!" One construction-and-other-trades panel member went so far as to describe the situation as "a nightmare. People were offering everything and stuff was coming from everywhere. I didn't know who had what, where it was, or how to get it to where it was needed if I did know where it was." Because of the sheer size of the site, logistics at the Trade Center had to be divided into multiple zones to make it possible to stage supplies near enough to workers.

> The OSHA [Occupational Safety and Health Administration] Manhattan-area office was destroyed in Building Six of World Trade . . . we were just trying to gear up with PPE. The first day we had ordered a bunch of personal protective equipment from Cincinnati, but with air traffic being out, couldn't fly it in. So we were considering even military transport to get it in to us. Finally, somebody volunteered a truck and got it into New Jersey and we were able to hike it across from Jersey to New York.
>
> *—Federal-and-state-agency panel member*

In the case of the September 11 attacks, responses were hampered by collateral developments. The arrival in New York City of FEMA's Urban Search and Rescue (USAR) teams, emergency supplies, and Incident Support Team (IST) was delayed for days by the grounding of commercial air transport. USAR task forces that did reach the area labored without their planned coordination and backup. "Everybody sat in airports, so there was no IST for two, three days," said one firefighter-special-operations panelist. "It had a big effect. The first time I talked to anybody on a FEMA radio off-site was on the third day because they just didn't get there."

Given the large number of responding agencies, communications and coordination became essential. Yet both mobile and land-line communication networks in lower Manhattan had been knocked out by the collapse of the World Trade Center. The remaining land lines and wireless networks were overwhelmed by high call volumes. One federal-and-state-agency panel member observed: "The cell tower that was in lower Manhattan was on top of the Trade

Center. So when the Trade Center went down, cellular phone communications went with it. When parts of the Trade Center went through the sidewalk and into the basement of the Verizon building, hard-line communications went with that."

> We were doing monitoring with special-ops groups with chemical agent and radiological [sensors]. But just the size of the structures, size of the whole complex, it took hours before we even got a good handle on the readings around the whole site.
>
> —*Firefighter-special-operations panel member*

In addition, the sheer scale of the incident made it very difficult to get information about the health and safety risks that were present. A major role of specialist firefighters, especially hazmat specialists, is risk assessment through the use of chemical-agent monitors and other assessment technologies. As one firefighter put it, "If your management system's working correctly, you can dish that off to your specialist people." At the World Trade Center, the New York City Fire Department (FDNY) lost much of its early reconnaissance capability when the firefighters and hazmat/special-operations personnel were killed in the building collapses. Afterwards, risk-assessment specialists reported having problems getting their equipment to work because of the amount of smoke and dust, which caused a large number of false readings. And even when people were available to do it, gathering data was difficult because of the large size of the disaster site.[2]

When the autumn 2001 anthrax episode is considered in total, the multiple individual responses also represent a large-scale event. The thousands of "white-powder events" and "anthrax rides" imposed significant manpower, equipment, and logistics burdens on emergency-response units across the country.

MULTIPLE THREATS, MULTIPLE EVENTS

Occupational safety and health hazards are associated with many emergencies, including structural fires and hazardous-materials spills. The hazards encountered in responding to the terrorism incidents included fire, falling debris, explosions, burning fuel, hazardous materials, structures prone to collapse, heat stress, exhaustion, and respiratory irritants. What made the responses to the terrorist events at the Murrah Federal Building, the Pentagon, and the World Trade Center more complicated was the presence of so many hazards, making them "multithreat events." Moreover, responders to a suspected terrorist inci-

---

[2]In contrast, at the Pentagon, where the smoke and fire-gases were less intense, the equipment performed appropriately.

The scale of a terrorist event can have a psychological impact and erode procedures, as indicated by the following comments made by firefighters at the NIOSH/RAND conference:

—All we were worried about was getting our guys out. Our main concern was to get guys out. Even a paper mask didn't matter to us.

—From what I saw in New York, at least the first week there, these guys went through something that was just unimaginable, and they didn't really care one bit about their own safety, their own health, they just didn't care. It wasn't part of their equation. The guys just worked and worked and worked and had no regard whatsoever for their own safety. They cared about the guy next to them. They didn't care about themselves at all. They just didn't care.

—The World Trade Center was such an enormous event that it caused, at least in our minds, you to weigh hazards. Our first concern was having something fall on us. So you start assessing real immediate mechanical hazards: "This building could still collapse. The thing on top of [Building] Five may fall." That overshadows concerns about carbon monoxide because it's in the immediate.

—We found that the atmospheric issues were so huge, you would have to back up to the river to get out of them. So the nature of the magnitude of the event causes almost a reweighing of what you consider normal limits. You couldn't begin to move into [an area] safe from carbon monoxide, we couldn't find one.

—I just have this image of everybody sitting there with these red flashing lights [from their carbon monoxide monitors] and the attitude was, "Where are you going to go? There's nowhere to go." I think it has an effect on the psychology, it starts to erode some of your procedures.

dent must be prepared for a host of additional potential threats, including secondary explosive devices and chemical, biological, and radioactive contaminants. Such possibilities dramatically complicate both hazard assessment and personal protection requirements. Said one special operations panel member, "When you have all the hazards lumped together, nothing out there will [protect against] everything. There's nothing that's good."

Numerous hazards associated with the terrorist attacks were singled out as being particularly unique or severe:

- Large amounts of unburned jet fuel at the Pentagon presented an explosion and toxic-substance hazard.
- At the World Trade Center site, welders inadvertently ignited a store of ammunition.[3] The resulting explosion sent shrapnel flying and injured workers. In another case, a utility worker was burned when he came in contact with a live 14-kilovolt power line.

[3]Several law-enforcement agencies shared an ammunitions depot within the World Trade Center.

> In a collapse like this, you have so many unusual situations. We had jet fuel, we had battery acid, asbestos, products of combustion, lead paint, silica, biological—things that are all okay individually when you run into them. When you throw them into a collapse environment where you really don't know how much, what's broken open, what's not, what's mixed, what it's touched, what hasn't—all those things aren't that simple to just sort out. Some of the people wanted to come in their specialty areas and say, "Well, let me tell you about this." [One might ask,] "Well, what does it do when it's affected with that?" "Well, I really don't know." So these things aren't quite as pigeonholed [in this situation] as they are sometimes.
>
> *—Firefighter-special-operations panel member*

- At the Pentagon, mold and mildew growth fueled by water from extended firefighting efforts presented a health hazard. There were also serious explosion and electrical hazards that extended beyond the initial response.

Several other hazards associated with the terrorist attacks were cited repeatedly in the conference discussions; these are briefly outlined below.

Rubble and Debris

One of the most striking hazards at the World Trade Center was the large pile of rubble and debris. A great deal of rubble and debris also was encountered in the vicinity of the Murrah Federal Building and inside the Pentagon, where many offices in and near the impact zone were being used to store office furniture and equipment.

> We had an incredible amount of debris inside the Pentagon from the jet fuel burning. It dropped all the ceilings and walls. They all dropped into the corridors. So we had a four-foot, five-foot-high pile of debris to crawl over to actually do any firefighting. There were a lot of hazards there.
>
> *—Firefighter-special-operations panel member*

Firefighters in particular were not familiar with such an environment: "Some of our folks were getting hung up on rebar, cutting themselves up," said one. Shifting or unstable rubble could cause strains or sprains or, worse, could result in trapped feet. Most work boots used by construction workers provide only limited ankle support, increasing the potential for turned or sprained ankles. The rubble pile at the World Trade Center also hampered efforts to protect workers against falls because there were no tie-off points to secure the ropes and harnesses. A typical building has many places to secure ropes, some designed specifically for that purpose (e.g., for window washers). But the rubble pile did not.

Emergency responders had only limited tools for removing rubble and debris. Indeed, initial debris removal at the World Trade Center was done by bucket brigade. Therefore, heavy construction equipment and crews had to be brought in immediately. The presence of heavy construction equipment on the scenes presented hazards to those in the vicinity, as well as to the equipment operators, who had to cope with tight quarters, uneven surfaces, and poor visibility.

> We found out what a powerful force gravity is. Everything was completely pulverized. You saw gray dirt, which was pulverized concrete, and you saw beams and you saw pipes, basically, with a lot of wires around. You didn't see anything identifiable beyond those three things, and pieces of paper every place. You didn't see a chair, a desk, a computer screen. I never saw a piece of glass the whole time I was there.
>
> *—Firefighter-special-operations panel member*

Dust and Smoke

Dust and smoke were a pervasive hazard at the World Trade Center—suppression efforts notwithstanding, the air in Lower Manhattan was filled with particulates for weeks after the attack. Particulates also were cited as a problem, although to a lesser extent, at the Pentagon and the Murrah Federal Building. Yet according to participants, the available protective equipment did not shield them from the risk. "I was sick for a month after I got back from Oklahoma City, and it's the same stuff—concrete dust," said one responder.[4]

According to data presented to the trades panel, respiratory injuries were reported frequently at the World Trade Center site, with almost 1,000 occurring in the first nine weeks.[5] Many more may emerge, it was argued, because those injuries caused by inhaling toxic fumes may not display symptoms for some time. In addition, available eye protection reportedly did not work well, resulting in numerous eye injuries. In the first week, 346 people were treated for eye

---

[4]According to press reports in late December 2001, as many as 500 New York firefighters who worked at the site were on leave for respiratory-related illnesses. As of January 2002, the Uniformed Firefighters Association estimated that about one-third of its 9,000 members suffered from the so-called "World Trade Center cough."

[5]*World Trade Center (WTC) Worker Injury and Illness Surveillance Update.*

injuries of all types. By the middle of the tenth week, the number exceeded 1,000.[6] Indeed, this was the second largest category of injury reported, accounting for 12 percent of all reported injuries.[7]

According to conference participants, ensuring that the right respirator was available, properly prescribed and fitted, and actually worn by the responder as prescribed posed enormous logistics, training, and management challenges in all of the responses to the terrorist attacks.

Heat

Intense heat—caused in part by the burning of thousands of gallons of jet fuel—was a concern at the World Trade Center and the Pentagon. Intense fires also burned in buildings adjacent to the twin towers—for example, Seven World Trade Center and Ninety West Street—but the FDNY had only limited personnel, equipment, and water to fight them. The heat intensity at the Pentagon was exacerbated, participants noted, by the concrete and slate roof and the bombproof windows, which limited the ability of firefighters to ventilate the structure. "The heat inside the Pentagon was like being in a brick oven." Some of the firefighters who encountered the intense heat were burned even before seeing the fire, noted special-operations personnel.

At the World Trade Center, the ground was hot because of burning material that continued to smolder for weeks.[8] Indeed, the rubble pile was so hot in places that it melted the soles of work boots. Companies donated supplies of work shoes, and construction workers laboring on the hotter parts of the rubble pile reportedly went through a pair a day. A boot wash was established where workers could cool their feet, but ultimately that simply traded one problem for another: Wet boots resulted in serious blisters. In the federal-and-state-agency panel, it was noted that USAR teams were usually the only responder units with gear appropriate for extended use in a hot rubble pile.

In general, the high-heat environment taxed the stamina of emergency responders, who often were suited up in heavy protective garments and labored for long periods without breaks or equipment changes.

---

[6]Ibid.

[7]The largest injury category was "Other," which accounted for 26 percent of the injuries. This category included such items as chapped lips, fatigue, and follow-up care (*World Trade Center Worker Injury and Illness Surveillance Update*).

[8]On December 19, 2001, the *New York Times* announced that the fires at the World Trade Center were finally extinguished.

Anthrax

Even though the range of risks at the Murrah Federal Building, the Pentagon, and the World Trade Center was broad, the risks were, at least separately, familiar. Anthrax was a different story. Responders did not know what or where the hazards were: "You can't measure the risks and do risk assessment, [so] you don't know what personal protection you need." With anthrax (or other biological agents), it is difficult to assess where emergency response starts and where it ends. Said one law-enforcement official, "The unknown is the big challenge, the invisible hazards." These problems were accentuated by the fact that the number of false alarms made it difficult to determine which anthrax-related incidents were truly hazardous and which were not.

High levels of uncertainty surrounded the responses to the anthrax episodes in autumn 2001, making the appropriate personal protection strategies difficult to execute, said several members of the law-enforcement and health-and-safety panels at the conference:

—One thing my team noticed when we went to treat a postal worker was that the information kept changing daily as to what the recommendations were. And how do you treat them, how do you protect them?

—The main challenge for hazard assessment at the anthrax sites was getting accurate information on the nature of the risks. The other difference is that at the World Trade Center we could identify the source of the contamination. But with the exposure to anthrax, it was [like] looking everywhere at the same time.

—The problem is, you can't assess the damage by just being there, like you can with something else. With the World Trade Center, you know what you have. It's totally different [with anthrax]. You're not even sure if you have a problem when you get a call for anthrax in the post office. . . . You can't see the hazards you're dealing with.

Stress

Firefighters and other emergency responders follow the principle: "Risk a life to save a life." However, in the aftermath of the terrorist attacks, the intensity of responders' work, the long duration of the response campaigns, the multiplicity of risks, the horrifying outcomes of the attacks, and the lack of knowledge about hazards all contributed to stress.

At the World Trade Center, many of the victims recovered were horribly mangled, and in many cases only parts of bodies were recovered. As one trades panel member put it, "Many of these workers had never seen a dead person—not in an automobile accident, not even in a funeral home." It was reported on the trades panel that over 100 cases of psychological stress among construction and trades personnel were treated during the first nine weeks at the World

Trade Center. However, the consensus of the panel was that many, many more experienced such stress but did not seek treatment. Conference participants noted that psychological risk for responders remains an understudied hazard.

> We had body temperatures at night of 104, 105 degrees that were coming out of [the Pentagon]. We had people who actually succumbed to seizure-related heat exhaustion. The heat exhaustion was due to the extensive, excessive heat that was in the building, and long carries of hose and long carries of equipment with the very heavy equipment they were wearing. They were in it until their bottles would run out, and then they'd have this long retreat. In the rescue mode, they would change [air bottles], and go back in. They worked until they dropped.
>
> *—Emergency-medical-services panel member*

Stress could affect responders' judgment about their own health and safety. A public health panelist commented, "[There's] almost hysteria with the anthrax group. . . . People get very scared and start asking 'Was I exposed?' and treating themselves." Such a response can be detrimental to a responder's health, since treatments for biological and chemical agents can have serious side effects. The stress can also cause responders to disregard their own health and safety. For example, one firefighter at the World Trade Center reported, "I had guys that needed medical attention that didn't get it for two or three weeks." An anecdote related on the federal-and-state-agency panel was similar: "One guy who was using a gas-powered cutting saw refused to give up to the point where the carbon monoxide dropped him. [He] didn't even want to hand off the tool. It was a semi-confined area. Just ran him down until he collapsed and they took him out."

> *The high-stress environment at the World Trade Center, combined with personal and professional bonds led to greater risk-taking during the response campaign, as indicated by this exchange on the firefighter panel:*
>
> Q: Do you think [if] you had more information about the hazards and the effects on you that you would be more careful in the risks?
>
> A: No. We have known it for years.
>
> A: No. No matter what you had in front of you, you were seeing one thing. In, recover, get them out.
>
> Q: Does it change somewhere after several days where there is a determination made that there probably isn't anybody else alive?
>
> A: You had to pry people off the piles for the first two or three weeks. You had to pry them off the pile.
>
> A: Because you had hopes that there was going to be someone in there.

CRIME-SCENE DESIGNATION

Another characteristic that distinguishes the terrorist incidents from most other large-scale disasters is the terrorist-attack sites are crime scenes. While some fires may be the result of arson and may thus require evidence collection, massive disasters such as hurricanes and earthquakes do not. Designation as a crime scene means that the number of groups requiring access increases and the nature of the activities that take place on-site changes. For example, emergency crews need to worry about preserving evidence. This can have important consequences for protecting the health and safety of emergency responders.

> When it's a weapon of mass destruction, hazardous material is the weapon. It's my crime scene. I don't want you to come and wash it away or police it up. I want you to leave it there so that I can perform my law-enforcement function—collecting and analyzing and trying to figure out who put it there.
>
> —*Law-enforcement panel member*

OFF-DUTY AND VOLUNTEER INVOLVEMENT

The United States has been identified historically and culturally as a nation of volunteers and citizens who provide mutual assistance in times of need. The terrorist attacks proved this. The psychological shock, combined with the large number of deaths and injuries involving emergency responders, resulted in a massive outpouring of community and volunteer involvement in the responses.

During the Oklahoma City, World Trade Center, and Pentagon events, many off-duty EMS, police, and fire personnel responded directly to the scenes, as did private ambulance services, doctors, and nurses. Many traveled hours to reach a site. Most volunteers arrived at the scenes without adequate PPE or radio communications, and they operated outside the direction of the incident commander, yet were willing to enter extremely hazardous locations. Such activity adds to the confusion and compounds the safety and rescue responsibilities of firefighters and other responders who are in the command structure. In the process, both off-duty volunteers and emergency responders may be subjected to greater danger from threats such as a collapse or other secondary events. It was pointed out that a volunteer nurse was killed by falling debris in the Oklahoma City response. As summed up by one special-operations panelist: "We appreciated all the help, but, I don't want to sound . . . it was a huge problem."

> [The volunteers were] a lot of well-intentioned people that didn't know what they were doing. They were just confusing the situation because they were operating outside of the chain of command, or outside of their knowledge.
>
> —*Firefighter panel member*

Very quickly, community and religious organizations, local businesses, and concerned citizens set up and staffed ad hoc catering, rest, and comfort stations near the disaster sites. Over time, political leaders, high-ranking government officials, and other public figures visited the terrorist sites to view the damage, support the responders, and console the bereaved. This forced emergency responders into new roles—trying to manage large numbers of community volunteers, well-wishers, and onlookers—for which they had few guidelines and little practice.

NEW ROLES, NEW RISKS

The scale of the terrorist events, their duration, and the range of hazards they presented required that many emergency responders take on atypical tasks for which they were insufficiently equipped or trained.

> We've changed the roles of special-ops groups over the years to include hazmat, confined space, high angle, and we've outfitted them. But now we're looking at regular front-line firefighters having a different role or responsibility or response and we may have to provide them with the proper PPE for that type of work.
>
> —*Firefighter-special-operations panel member*

Structural fires typically involve fire suppression and rescue, and fire departments have well-defined and carefully honed standard operating procedures and PPE for those activities. For responders at the World Trade Center, conditions in the rubble pile were unique: There were very few voids. This reduced opportunities for primary reconnaissance, shoring and stabilization, void searches, and rescue—important tasks in a large structural fire.[9] The number of injured who required extrication, triage, and treatment was relatively small: "Either you were dead or you walked away from it. There was very little in between," observed one special-operations responder that was at the scene. "There really was not that much to do." The experience at the Pentagon was

[9]Void searches and building stabilization and shoring were undertaken in partially damaged and collapsed buildings adjacent to the twin towers as well as at the Murrah Federal Building and the Pentagon.

similar, with firefighters commenting that the evacuation consisted of the initial exit only; beyond that, there was "a lot of searching obviously but no rescue really." Conversely, firefighters became engaged in activities they usually do not do: "busting up and hauling concrete," scrambling over the rubble pile, and removing victims and decayed bodies and body parts.

In all of the terrorist-incident responses, EMS personnel were on-scene, performing rescue operations. Moreover, in every incident, EMS personnel were caring for patients in the rubble pile. Several additional groups of personnel—sanitation engineers, food-service workers, and construction workers—were deployed at the scenes and placed in hazardous environments. Classifying the site as a crime scene also had important implications for occupational health and safety: Few crime-scene investigators had had to contend with ongoing fire-suppression and rescue activities and thus had limited knowledge of possible risks.

From an historical perspective, the police have always been gun-toters . . . writing tickets. Terrorist acts with chem/bio and those types of things have always been secondary. Now there's great importance of the police getting more involved with special teams to respond to these types of [incidents], and we're kind of falling behind the curve. Fire and EMS have had these standards. Fire and EMS have been practicing. They carry their PPE with them, whereas the police don't. The only police organizations that really have this gear with them are the specialized teams.

—Law-enforcement panel member

Those EMS groups with fire department affiliation usually had some knowledge about rescue and hazard recognition, but many did not have access to the personal protective equipment they knew they needed. The typical construction worker arrived at the World Trade Center site wearing essentially street clothes—jeans and shirts or t-shirts. And with some exceptions (for example, welders), most construction workers did not wear protective garments during their shift. Construction workers have well-developed models for erecting buildings and, indeed, for destroying them. However, those models did not mesh well at the terrorist-attack sites because the planning and preparation that normally accompanies building demolitions (e.g., removal of hazardous materials, establishment of traffic patterns) did not occur or took a long time to implement.

To summarize, the definition and roles of an emergency responder expanded greatly in the wake of the terrorist attacks, but few responders had adequate personal protective equipment, training, or information for such circumstances.

Chapter Three

PERFORMANCE AND AVAILABILITY OF PERSONAL PROTECTIVE EQUIPMENT

At the conference, participants were asked to address a series of questions regarding the performance of personal protective equipment. The central concern was understanding how available PPE performed in protecting against the hazards present at the terrorist-incident sites and for the tasks emergency responders had to undertake over the duration of the campaign. Related concerns were whether responders had adequate supplies of PPE and what equipment maintenance measures were in effect.

PERFORMANCE

A theme that was repeated frequently throughout the conference was that available PPE technologies worked well at the terrorist-attack sites if they were employed as intended and for the hazards they were designed to protect against. "Everything worked well when it was used for what it was supposed to do," according to one participant.

But given the nature of the extended and complex response campaigns that followed the terrorist attacks, scrupulous use of equipment only for tasks for which it was designed proved difficult. Some standard-issue equipment that responders had and used was not designed to work in the types of environments presented by the terrorist incidents. Some equipment simply broke down. Helmet face shields and goggles were designed for impact and splash protection; they provided no protection against dust and particulates. Boots (especially rubber boots) were not fitted properly and melted in the high-heat environment. Some of the available hearing protection was designed for high-impact noise such as sirens, not for the constant lower-frequency noise from heavy-duty equipment to which personnel were exposed. When responding to anthrax incidents, responders did not know whether their respirators were adequate. They reported that such shortcomings, coupled with the perception that marginally effective PPE was hindering their ability to do their jobs—and was even inducing other risks—led them frequently to do without personal protection as they sought to carry out their pressing missions.

> Firefighting equipment is designed well for firefighting operations that typically last 30 minutes, 40 minutes, or an hour. But when you have fires burning for six, eight, nine weeks, bunker gear gets to be pretty cumbersome.
>
> —*Firefighter-special-operations panel member*

The following discussion summarizes observations made about key categories of personal protective equipment. However, it should be noted that, as one firefighter-special-operations panelist emphasized, the way it all goes together and interfaces is as important as the capabilities of individual pieces of equipment.

Respiratory Protection

Of all personal protective equipment, respiratory protection elicited the most extended discussion across all of the professional panels, because airborne hazards—such as airborne particulates, toxic gases, and anthrax spores—were present in all the terrorist events and because the respiratory system is commonly known as the primary pathway for hazardous exposure. Moreover, responders did not (and, to some extent, still do not) know which airborne hazards were present at the terrorist scenes.[1] Another reason for the concern with respiratory protection is that respiratory technologies and the procedures guiding their use tend to be more involved and complex than those for other equipment such as gloves and footwear.

> The only way you could theoretically keep anybody from getting a pulmonary exposure in these events is to keep them on an SCBA 24 hours a day for the duration of the event, which is absolutely impossible. So you're going to get exposed, no matter what. It's just a matter of how much of an exposure you're going to take on.
>
> —*Firefighter-special-operations panel member*

Panel members discussed the merits of several types of respiratory gear and, within types, several variants. For example, an SCBA was seen as providing the best protection for fire suppression, but it offers only a short-term supply of

[1]From September to December 2001, media reports pointed to uncertainties about environmental quality at the World Trade Center site. For example, it was suggested that asbestos used in construction might have been pulverized too finely to be detected using standard measurement techniques.

fresh air—up to one hour, depending on the bottle. Another drawback identified was the heavy weight of the SCBA ensemble. Limited air supply and heavy weight were seen as significant limitations by firefighting and special-operations personnel working at the Pentagon, given the long travel distances involved in getting to the fire zone.[2] Lightweight carbon-fiber bottles that some squads have acquired recently were said to be a significant improvement: "That worked well," concluded one special operations firefighter. In any case, most teams lack sufficient refill capacity to keep responders supplied. In Oklahoma City, this situation forced responders to revert to APRs, even when suspected airborne contaminants called for the use of an SCBA.

For situations where fire-related gases were not present, the firefighter panel preferred lighter-weight APRs to their SCBAs. And while one department reported using modular respirator cartridges that were compatible with their SCBA masks, most panelists complained that full-face respirators reduced their field of vision at best and fogged up at worst. Several of the firefighters at the World Trade Center who inhaled large quantities of dust during the collapse of the towers opted for paper masks because they felt that any increased respiratory burden of breathing through an APR was too much. Said one, "I am congested enough, why do I need more restriction on my face?" This led a firefighter from the Pentagon to suggest that powered air-purifying respirators (PAPRs) would have made it easier to breathe and would have reduced fogging. However, their significantly higher cost meant that few companies had them: "Obviously we didn't use those. You would need [to acquire] hundreds and hundreds of those types."

Many respirators were uncomfortable, causing many wearers to use them only intermittently or to discard them after short periods. Referring to the common habit of removing respirators and hanging them around the neck, one federal-and-state-agency panelist quipped, "There were a lot of neck protectors . . . Adam's apples were all very clean." Even paper dust masks, which offered minimal respiratory protection, were often seen hanging around workers' necks because they chafed the bridge of the nose.

A general criticism of currently available respirator systems is that they are made by different manufacturers and have different fittings. Thus, air tanks and canisters often are not interchangeable. This is particularly the case with more specialized, narrow-spectrum PPE. A lack of interoperability poses signif-

---

[2] A plenary speaker stated that while bottles may have a maximum "rated time" of up to 60 minutes, his research indicated that the effective supply lasts less than half that time, depending on levels of exertion. The time needed to safely enter and exit a hazardous location further reduces the effective interval.

> [The respirator] was uncomfortable. I was afraid it didn't have a good seal, so I broke the seal. I spent about 20 hours at the scene. I wore a P-100 with those little cartridges. I still was uncomfortable, I kept going like this [*gestures with back and forth motion like a trombone player*], fooling around with it. I kept saying to myself, "I don't know how those folks working in the pile, doing heavy labor, could do it with any type of mask."
>
> —*Health-and-safety panel member*

icant problems during an extended campaign. When outside supplies are brought in—for example, from neighboring jurisdictions, federal caches, or manufacturers—responders often have to wait for their own logistics teams to arrive and distribute backup supplies that will work with their equipment. "If that's the case," one officer said, "I might as well stay home." Responders on the EMS and firefighter panels also reported spending a lot of time trying to match up respirator parts, and some went without respiratory protection because they could not find the proper components.

> The problem that I saw from being there . . . was people would bring in respirators but they would only bring in half of it. They wouldn't bring in the cartridges, or they'd bring in just what they had on scene. And these would get distributed in certain ways, but we were having a real tough time just matching everything up.
>
> —*Firefighter-special-operations panel member*

A related concern had to do with confusion over certification. Responders familiar with respirators are trained to use only models with a certification stamp, but they found that available respirators often lacked any such stamp, even though the packaging sometimes indicated certification. This led to confusion over whether the respirators should be used. It was unclear whether this was a result of expedited respirator production or a change in certification procedures.

> [A respirator] has to be comfortable and noninhibitive. From a supervisor's point of view, I have to be able to talk to my guys. If I [sound like] "blah blah blah," then five times a day I'm pulling it off just to tell them something. Next thing you know, it comes off one time and it doesn't go back on.
>
> —*Firefighter-special-operations panel member*

Respirators make it difficult for people to communicate, and as a result, many wearers broke their seals in order to talk. This is an important problem, particularly in the early stages of response to a terrorist attack, when access to accurate information is most crucial: Workers need to be able to warn their colleagues about dangers, such as falling objects, and supervisors need to be able to communicate with their teams. Special-operations panelists were particularly concerned about such communication problems, especially with the less-expensive respirator models provided at the terrorist-attack sites. Communication continues to be a problem in the sustained phase, when responders want to take a break, or in high-noise environments, when workers pull their masks down to talk over the noise, inhaling contaminants in the process.

The full-face respirator worked the best. As a hazmat team member, I have a full-face respirator. So when everybody else was looking for dust masks, the hazmat team was slapping cartridges on their full-face, and they could handle just about everything. We had voice amplifiers where we could communicate. If they had just a half-face from [retail stores], their communications went down quickly.

—Firefighter-special-operations panel member

No respirator is NIOSH-certified for protection against anthrax, and there are no established selection criteria for respirators to use in responses to anthrax incidents.[3] As a result, emergency responders improvised. Powered air-purifying respirators were seen as effective protection against inhaling spores as long as the filter cartridge was in good condition and maintained filtered air blowing on the face. Special-operations personnel expressed concerns that respirators fitted with a high-efficiency particulate air (HEPA) filter—originally considered adequate—might not be effective for small-particle, military-grade anthrax. Panelists also indicated that how and when they used respiratory protection varied by incident. Sometimes they would don the mask before entering a building; at other times, they waited until they got near a specific room. Because of the large number of hoaxes and false alarms, PPE use often depended on informal judgments made prior to arrival at the scene about the credibility of an incident.

Garments

As was the case with SCBAs, the clothing that on-duty firefighters typically wore to the terrorist scenes often was too heavy for the extended campaigns and heavy labor (e.g., hauling concrete on 12-hour shifts) they had to perform. First-response firefighters arrived at the World Trade Center and the Pentagon in standard structural-fire turnout gear—heavy bunker pants and coat. In the

[3]NIOSH has recently released *Interim Recommendations for the Selection and Use of Protective Clothing and Respirators Against Biological Agents,* a guide that addresses respiratory protection against anthrax threats (available at http://www.cdc.gov/niosh/unp-intrecppe.htm).

high-heat environments of these sites, the suits' limited breathability and extra weight contributed to fatigue and heat stress as the firefighters performed demanding physical labor. Furthermore, after firefighters had been on the scene for an extended time, the layers of their garments often became compressed from sweat on the inside or water penetration (e.g., through the boot-pant interface), leading to reduced thermal protection capacity. Once the inside of a garment was damp, reexposure to heat sometimes led to steam burns.

Members of the firefighter panel who were present at the World Trade Center, the Pentagon, and the Murrah Federal Building said that their bunker gear worked well during firefighting and for the initial response, but they agreed that other types of gear would be useful for situations where there is no risk of fire. Several special-operations personnel said that they never used full bunker gear during the emergency responses because of problems with overheating and the difficulty of maneuvering in the rubble pile. Accordingly, many reported that they modified or improvised on the basis of their personal assessment of the situation and what worked best for themselves. Some wore battle dress uniforms (BDUs, also known as military fatigues), which had the benefit of being lighter and more flexible for working in confined spaces but lacked the greater thermal and abrasion protection of bunker gear. "I'm on the dive team," said one firefighter. "What I wore initially was my military jungle boots, my dive coveralls, a fire department helmet."

> Most of the equipment we have is designed for one hazard, not multiple hazards. Bunker gear works well in the fire situation for thermal [protection], but when you're working in a collapse situation, BDUs work better because you're moving around. We also had a couple of USAR team members get burned when they had pockets of gas ignite around them and they were not wearing thermal protection.
>
> *—Firefighter-special-operations panel member*

On the other hand, BDUs also did not provide adequate protection against biological threats such as those present when responders encountered decomposing bodies during their excavations. One firefighter mentioned that during their work at the World Trade Center site, two co-workers received minor cuts they did not specifically treat. Both individuals later developed serious infections, possibly because of the biological threats at the site, and they had to be hospitalized.

Most PPE is not designed or manufactured with the law-enforcement mission in mind, panelists said. The fit and performance of biohazard garments were of particular concern to law-enforcement representatives. Tyvek™ suits are not small enough to properly accommodate many female officers, and they are not large enough for some male officers. In addition, there is no uniformity in sizing among vendors. An XL-size garment from one manufacturer may be the equivalent to an XXL from another. Suits also need to be better reinforced at the joints to prevent them from tearing when officers bend or kneel down to pick up evidence at a site. Moreover, law-enforcement officers must be made aware that once the seal is broken on the packaging of a suit, the suit has a service life of only 60 to 90 days.[4] Finally, suits with heat-sealed seams were viewed as providing better protection than those with sewn seams. During decontamination, for example, one participant reported leakage through sewn seams—the bleach solution had seeped through to a t-shirt worn underneath the suit in the same areas as the seams. This gave rise to concerns that anthrax spores may have also seeped through the seams. Another officer had assumed that in buying a coated suit, he was buying one that was liquid-resistant. Indeed, the fabric was liquid-resistant, but the sewn seams were not, again giving rise to worries of possible contamination.

Health and safety responders working at anthrax sites found that their hazmat suits were superior to those worn by FBI responders; the latter were extremely heavy and did not allow sufficient freedom of movement. Apparently the FBI suits also caused heavy sweating, to the point that agents' gloves filled with perspiration. Federal and state agency panelists cited the same shortcomings of Tyvek™ suits and also noted that Tyvek™ suits have poor resistance to abrasion and they tear easily.

Footwear

At both the Pentagon and the World Trade Center, firefighters' boots became soaked because the seams failed in hot water or water came in over the sides. In addition, at the World Trade Center, the rubble pile was so hot in places that it melted the soles of boots (a problem noted by members of the trades, law-enforcement, and firefighter panels). Work shoes with steel reinforcements in the soles and toes protected feet against punctures by sharp objects but often could not be worn because they conducted and retained the heat, causing blistered or scorched feet. One special-operations member said, "Steel toes never break in. We'd all be sitting there at night bandaging up and everybody had the same blisters. It was related to wearing the steel toe for that duration."

> Wearing fire boots for 40 hours straight is not good for your feet. . . . They're not designed for that long of use. They're designed for quick 30 minutes, 45 minutes, hour firefights. They're not designed for working piles and walking on steel.
>
> —*Firefighter-special-operations panel member*

---

[4]After that time period, the suit's ability to protect declines.

Members of the law-enforcement panel noted that they have access to boots as part of their standard uniform. Less-expensive boots do not last long, however. Some officials reported using more-expensive brands (e.g., Danners, Matterhorns) that offered a greater range of protection and more comfort over longer intervals, but they cost up to $300 per pair. At the World Trade Center site, even the expensive boots frequently had to be discarded because they became contaminated with the biological and chemical materials in the water around the site.

> My feet were blistered and bloody by the second day because [I was] wearing leather boots soaking wet, and there was nothing I could do.
>
> —*Firefighter panel member*

To protect boots from contamination at both the Pentagon and Trade Center attack sites, latex or Tyvek™ overbooties were often used, but the law-enforcement panel commented on the difficulties of putting latex booties on over their work boots. For example, a size 13 latex overbootie should ideally fit over a size 13 boot, but up to three people may be needed to get the bootie over the boot (one to hold down the boot, the other two to put on the bootie). Panelists questioned the durability of overbooties, remarking that some types are not durable and get torn up almost as quickly as they are put on. The law-enforcement panel also questioned whether latex overbooties had been subjected to any form of testing or certification.

> An industrial hygienist showed me her work boots, and the soles were dissolved off. So you really don't know what you're going to step into sometimes. It had just eaten through the bottom of the soles.
>
> —*Federal-and-state-agency panel member*

Gloves

Structural firefighting gloves worked well until they got wet and hardened, which further reduced their limited dexterity. As the law-enforcement panel noted, gloves should be well-fitted and flexible enough to pick up small items, but at the same time, they should protect against piercing and contamination. This is crucial, said one participant: "Sometimes you have to stick your hand in some very strange places to pick up evidence." If an extender is not available to perform this reaching function, officers often use their bare hands. Maintaining manual dexterity was also of concern to special-operations representatives.

For construction-trades workers, gloves with leather or Kevlar reinforcing worked well to protect hands, and most workers wore them. However, leather gloves were cited by special-operations personnel as a particular risk in terms of both biological and chemical hazards, since leather can wick in and retain contaminants dissolved in the water that is prevalent on-site. This view was reiterated by members of the health-and-safety panel, who observed that rescue workers at the World Trade Center did not consistently protect their hands against potential hazards from human remains and bodily fluids. Biohazard protective glove liners were seldom used inside heavy dugout gloves. Cotton gloves also were deemed ineffective because they rapidly fell apart when workers were handling abrasive debris.

Eyewear

A large number of eye injuries at the World Trade Center reportedly stemmed from the type of eye protection distributed on-site, said a member of the trades panel. Safety glasses were readily available, but they did not protect against the most prevalent hazard, airborne particles. They worked reasonably well in protecting the eye against trauma injury and fluid splashes, which is what they are designed to do. However, the sides of the glasses are open, allowing dust to enter eyes and to irritate them. Heavy labor in hot weather, which caused dehydration and dry eyes, apparently compounded this problem at the sites.

Wraparound sunglasses were used for eye protection by law-enforcement workers at the World Trade Center site because of harsh glare and reflections of the sun. But they reported difficulties wearing any kind of eye protection in low-light conditions, because of poor visibility.

Safety goggles also were provided at the World Trade Center, and these apparently worked better for keeping dust out of workers' eyes. However, law-enforcement personnel and firefighters reported that goggles were not comfortable, hindered peripheral vision, and tended to fog—especially "anti-fog" models issued by the U.S. Government Services Administration. Better anti-fog goggles were distributed at the World Trade Center during the sustained response. Trades and law-enforcement panelists reported that some goggles were not compatible or did not fit well with half-face respirators. Training reportedly helped reduce the likelihood that respirators would become dislodged.

Full-face visors were also available, and these too helped keep dust out of eyes. They were not as effective in this regard as the goggles, but they appeared to be more comfortable to wear.

All eye protection equipment suffered from scratched lenses, and only limited facilities were available for rinsing eyewear at the World Trade Center site.

Trades workers reported simply wiping their eyewear off, which scratched the lenses.

Hearing Protection

Hearing protection became an issue during the sustained response phase, when heavy equipment was brought in to break up and clear away rubble and debris. Earplugs were readily available at the World Trade Center site, as they are on most construction sites. Panel members familiar with the construction trades indicated that workers were accustomed to the hearing protection provided and tended to use it when required. The challenge was to obtain the proper level of protection: "You're trying to muffle some sounds but still hear your radios," observed one special-operations panelist. Law-enforcement officials at the World Trade Center reported being less inclined to wear hearing protection because they needed to be able to hear their radios as well as voices or tapping when they were searching for survivors.

Head Protection

Head protection appeared to work well at the attack sites. Construction workers, for example, routinely wore hard hats, which provided reasonable protection against typical hazards.

> You can't wear the fire helmets we have for more than an hour . . . your neck! I used to be 5'10"; I'm 5'8" now! I tried to wear it for three hours. I noticed that throughout [the response] people were in danger zones holding up their hats with their arm.
>
> —*Emergency-medical-services panel member*

Standard firefighter helmets offered effective protection against a broad range of threats. Some panelists questioned their usefulness in the responses to the terrorist attacks, however, given the long duration of operations (the weight of a standard fire helmet is difficult to endure for more than an hour) and the nature of the hazards present. Regarding other types of commercially available helmets, one law-enforcement official observed, "Most come unassembled, and it took a PhD in engineering to figure out how to put the helmet together." Chinstraps are not well suited for use by responders who are wearing respirators. Another complaint was that good-quality helmets have little or no air circulation, which can lead to overheating. Even so, many firefighters at the World Trade Center site wore their fire helmets for several weeks for identification purposes.

Special-operations panel members indicated that traditional fire helmets, which have a large brim to protect the back of the neck, are inappropriate for working in confined spaces. During confined-space operations, many special-operations personnel wear a smooth "kiwi" helmet without a brim; its smoother surface and tighter fit to the head help reduce the risk of getting snagged on protruding debris.

One useful accessory cited by the law-enforcement panel was the Pelican™ light (supplied a few days after the World Trade Center attack), which attaches to the helmet, providing hands-free illumination. The use of Pelican™ lights facilitated crawling around in dark spaces without having to carry a flashlight. Special-operations panel members cautioned, however, that mounted lights may get caught on debris. Therefore, some participants indicated that using lights that could be detached if they became caught (or if they needed to be aimed by hand) would be a better alternative.

AVAILABILITY AND SUITABILITY

For many firefighters at the conference, PPE availability (specifically, the ability to obtain or replace gear after the first day of the response) was as important a concern as PPE performance, especially at the World Trade Center. Some health-and-safety panelists expressed a similar view. For example, there was an acute shortage of respirators early on.[5] They felt that PPE supply shortages were less acute at the Pentagon and in the anthrax episodes.

At the World Trade Center, adequate supplies of personal protective equipment became available by the third or fourth day, as commercial air transport resumed and logistics capabilities improved, according to special-operations representatives. Other panelists indicated that adequate supplies of some equipment, including respirators, were not available until later—as much as seven to nine days later. Some responders complained that when equipment, such as boots, arrived, those who needed it were sometimes not able to get it because of a lack of proper inventory control. Also, the equipment that was issued, some observed, could be characterized as "one-size-fits-all," even when it didn't. The broad approach taken was intended to simplify PPE training and reduce interoperability problems, but it was not without drawbacks.

As we have seen, discussion participants in many panels questioned the suitability and quality of PPE—gloves, respirators, masks, goggles, and safety glasses—distributed on-site. One special-operations panelist described being

---

[5]The health-and-safety panelists themselves generally believed that they were well equipped for their needs, but the emergency responders they were serving and monitoring did not have adequate PPE.

handed a respirator out of a box and just being told, "Here's your respirator," with no other description of its capabilities. It turned out to be a quarter-face respirator with only the bare minimum of particulate filtration, a device that was inappropriate for his activities on the site. Another frequently criticized item was "hardware store variety" paper breathing masks that were available at the World Trade Center. A private-sector representative suggested that many firms sent equipment without considering whether it would be useful or not and, in some cases, sent products that had been sitting in their warehouses not selling. One firefighter at the World Trade Center said, "There was, literally, junk everywhere. Good intentions. . . . People sent crates after crates after crates of stuff they thought would be good to have in there." Although this may have been the PPE that was readily available to ship on short notice, having it on the scene reportedly did not measurably help the responders.

Attendees at the conference pointed out that members of different professional groups working side by side at the scene often used markedly different protective equipment because of differences in their professions' standard operations procedures, what was made available to them, or what they customarily wore to do their jobs. For example, law-enforcement panelists noted that there was a rush on all types of equipment, and because most law-enforcement agencies did not allocate enough funding to stockpile PPE, they ran out. A member of the law-enforcement panel working at the Pentagon site ran out of biohazard suits in 24 hours, but he was able to arrange for supplies from other federal agencies.

There are many types of respirators, but few are built with the law-enforcement mission in mind. Many law-enforcement officials wore military masks because they are more compatible with the law-enforcement mission (for instance, when a person is holding a rifle, the canister of a nonmilitary mask can get in the way). Yet, because NIOSH has not certified military masks, panelists indicated that they were uncomfortable issuing the masks to their officers and were concerned that they were violating compliance requirements. A specific brand of mask was referred to as being better because it could be used for four different applications and featured interchangeable parts. U.S. Capitol Police were fitted with these masks to investigate anthrax incidents.

A lack of adequate personal protective equipment was cited as a significant problem for many response organizations dealing with anthrax. Hazmat teams typically had suitable gear, but their personnel often were overtasked, given the large number of hoaxes and false alarms involving powdery substances thought to be anthrax. Firefighters and police officers, on the other hand, usually lacked sufficient PPE and training to respond safely. Of the law-enforcement officials participating in the NIOSH/RAND conference, postal inspectors contended that they had the least protection. A panel member reported that to investigate cases of anthrax, inspectors were issued a pair of latex gloves and a dust mask (which they later found out was completely ineffective) and were also offered the antibiotic Cipro™. At the end of the discussion, they expressed the desire to find out what kind of PPE could be made available to them as they inspect future cases of reported anthrax or other biological/chemical agents.

Given the large number of white-powder events, PPE supply became a problem for many emergency-responder units. At anthrax scenes, law-enforcement officers' standard-issue belts and boots had to be thrown away because their leather and canvas components were too porous and could not be properly decontaminated.

With the proliferation of "white-powder" and other threats posed by terrorists, front-line emergency responders are facing a much wider range of potential hazards for which they are ill-equipped, noted firefighter-special-operations panel members at the conference:

We had anthrax letters before this event. The special ops groups had powered air-purifying respirators or respirators on their apparatus to deal with [anthrax calls], as the recommended PPE. But when you get to a large event like this, we don't typically supply APRs or PAPRs to first-response firefighters. They did not have that.

We had [an anthrax] scare in our building. We were downstairs, so we suited up and went upstairs. When we got upstairs, PD was there, and they said, "Oh sorry, we took care of that already." They were just in their regular uniform and we were dressed up in PPE.

MAINTENANCE AND DECONTAMINATION

Many panel participants commented that personal protective equipment was being used and maintained incorrectly. Law-enforcement panelists noted that overtightening a mask could cause it to crack. At one terrorist attack site, 55-gallon barrels were seen being filled up with cracked masks that had to be thrown away. Safety officers realized that training the officers, even just saying, "It doesn't have to be so tight," could save a lot of masks. Federal and state agency representatives noted that respirator cartridges often were not replaced at the proper intervals. In some cases, cartridges were discarded after less than two hours of use (much less time than is appropriate), while in other cases, "a lot of workers would work for the whole week on one cartridge." This was sometimes due to the unavailability of replacement cartridges, while in other instances it had to do with not receiving or not following instructions on respirator use. By the second day of the responses at the World Trade Center and the Pentagon, firefighters observed that their boots, bunker gear, and gloves had become soaked. Although some panelists reported that their departments quickly issued them duplicate sets of certain equipment, most wore their wet equipment for days.

Firefighters and special-operations panelists expressed their concern that PPE decontamination efforts (the process of removing potentially hazardous material from personnel and equipment as they leave a site) were haphazard and not very effective. At the attack sites themselves, practical concerns got in the way of effective decontamination. Workers at the World Trade Center who had only a single set of protective clothing did not want the clothes wetted (any more) during decontamination, fearing that this would further reduce their comfort and mobility. A firefighter commented, "I had guys running around with the same gear on for three or four weeks before it even started to get cleaned." An EMS panel member went further: Some responders did not clean or decontaminate their turnout gear at all in the three months following September 11. "[Decontamination] takes the ensemble away from the employee, who then needs a new replacement ensemble," said another EMS panelist. One participant reported that his organization working at the Pentagon contracted a commercial service to have the work clothes of technical rescue and USAR personnel cleaned and dried while they were off their 12-hour shifts. The arrangement made a "big difference" because it reduced supply burdens, and workers returned to work in fresh gear.

Equipment designed to be reused was often discarded instead. Many noted that respirators were discarded well before the end of their designed service life, in part because users did not know the equipment capabilities. A special-operations panelist argued that, because of the large supply of air-purifying respirators available at the Pentagon, workers treated them as if they were disposable. Another said, "We were throwing respirators away, we didn't know how to clean them right." When workers took off their respirators for a break, they had no way to keep them clean. One special-operations panelist described his APR as "nothing but a cup sitting there under your chin" collecting dust that he would breathe into his lungs when he put the mask back on.

The large number of anthrax responses imposed significant burdens on decontamination regimes. Reusable hazmat gear was subject to high rates of wear and tear as suits were constantly put in service, decontaminated, and packed up again. Law-enforcement panelists noted that certain types of boots began cracking over time from being repeatedly soaked in a bleach solution and then dried. "You can't get better protection," a special-operations representative said of standard bunker gear and SCBA. However, because of decontamination problems, these should be worn only when confronting a "real anthrax situation."

> With sustained operations, I've seen some SCBAs that started out basically brand new and were ready to be thrown away in a month's time from the continuous [use of bleach]—deteriorating hoses, straps, metal parts.
>
> —*Firefighter-special-operations panel member*

Because of the problems of obtaining and decontaminating gear, several special-operations panelists indicated they had to modify the way they dressed for the growing number of anthrax calls. Initially, they responded in basic air-purifying respirators, but they had difficulty decontaminating them fast enough to keep up with the call volume. To solve the problem, they shifted to wearing a full SCBA inside a disposable Tyvek™ suit, since the outer layer could be discarded. One federal-and-state-agency panelist commented that Tyvek™ suits were in such short supply that responders asked if they could be reused. One special-operations panelist said, "The logistics and the number of calls began to drive the whole policy."[6]

Finally, participants on the firefighter and special-operations panels pointed out that communications and other devices that run on specialized batteries that are not readily available, rechargeable, or interchangeable are impractical for extended responses. Many of the flashlights in use by responders, for example, were powered by rechargeable battery packs that could be recharged only in a specialized unit back at the fire station. As a result, after the first 12 hours of response, the flashlights became essentially useless: "When we are on extended scenes, we are not able to recharge on the scene and reuse our gear." In the words of one firefighter, "The only thing that saved us was [a retail firm] coming in with a truckload of lights. I mean crates and crates of lights." Panel members indicated that rechargeable units were preferable to those using specialized batteries. They suggested that it would be better if such devices, whether they were rechargeable or not, accepted readily available disposable batteries such as D-cells. That way, power for a responder's equipment could be cached or would be available through local retail networks.

---

[6]Nevertheless, several firefighters and law-enforcement panelists were concerned about the "public-perception hit" that occurred when they transitioned from using only respirators to full suits and breathing apparatus. Several hazmat participants indicated that their leaders were also concerned about how the change would affect public fears about the situation.

Chapter Four

INFORMATION AND TRAINING

The discussions at the conference identified two fundamental issues concerning hazard assessment and information regarding personal protective equipment use: a lack of information about hazards and equipment, and inadequate management and communication of information.

HAZARD ASSESSMENT

Occupational health and safety hazards at the scenes were assessed in a variety of ways, according to conference participants. A primary method was direct observation, backed by personal experience: "First responders know the typical hazards," said one panelist.

> In the first two or three days, as far as levels of asbestos, silica, lead, any of the other metals that would have gone airborne, I have no clue . . . because we were denied access to the [World Trade Center] site. We were prepared to sample, but they said, "Thanks, but no thanks." About a week or so into the incident, when everybody started noticing that we finally had a chance to hang our sample pumps around, everybody started asking about what they were breathing the first couple of days. Couldn't tell them.
>
> —*Federal-and-state-agency panel member*

Such immediate assessments were supplemented by more formal and detailed hazard monitoring. Conference participants noted that there were many people, representing many different organizations engaged in monitoring, at the attack scenes. In some cases, the large number of agencies involved led to confusion—over who was authorized to engage in monitoring, what the appropriate monitoring standards were, and what the proper thresholds were. Another problem panelists reported was that data gathered were contradictory because each person and organization brought a different approach to hazard assessment and management. "Nobody agrees what is safe," noted a special-operations panelist, who also noted the lack of agreement about what the appropriate response should be. "There is no cookbook," said another.

According to special-operations personnel, problems with uncoordinated hazard assessment also existed at the Oklahoma City site.

RISK COMMUNICATION

Emergency responders repeatedly stressed the importance of having timely health and safety information. "Responders respond and they go to work right away, with or without information," stated a special-operations panelist. "What kills rescue responders is the unknown," commented an EMS panel member. "If you had the known, you should be hopefully prepared for it." The information must also be accurate, as one law-enforcement panelist warned: "With cops, it's a real simple mantra: 'If you don't give me information, I will give you a rumor.' And rumors will spread faster than information." Although many organizations and agencies were actively monitoring health and safety hazards at the terrorist-incident sites, problems in producing and disseminating hazard information reduced the effectiveness of their efforts.

Risk communication varied among the terrorist-attack sites. It reportedly took a week before coordinated daily briefings on the conditions at the World Trade Center site were conducted. Eventually, risk and hazard information was communicated to agency and team leaders through on-site daily meetings. At the World Trade Center and Pentagon sites, several different daily meetings were held covering issues such as safety and health, incident planning, and daily goals and activities. In addition, some agencies produced periodic "situation reports" for their staffs. At the same time, there was a sense among some panelists that the information often failed to get communicated to individual front-line responders or "across a number of organizations."

> At [the] World Trade Center, they did a great job in having safety meetings a couple of times a day, health meetings a couple of times a day. All the . . . subject matter experts were all brought in, issues were discussed. And all of the answers were there to the questions that they had at least asked to that point. The sampling material was there. These were the people that really had the good information relative to health and safety issues at a site. Where the breakdown was, what we did poorly, was to disseminate that information effectively over the entire field.
>
> *—Federal-and-state-agency panel member*

Several additional shortcomings were noted by conference participants. Special-operations and law-enforcement responders reported the problem of different information sources telling them different things. One participant related the following anecdote: A computer bank with a large backup battery power unit was located within the fire zone at the Pentagon. Initial guidance provided by USAR teams indicated that the batteries did not present a significant hazard, and responders had been working in and around them for 12 to 14 hours. Subsequent consultations with the private contractor engaged in the building's renovation indicated that the batteries should be treated as a hazard: "We isolated that area and didn't go in there." Speaking of the World Trade Center, another special-operations responder pointed to a series of waves of concerns, including fear of radioactivity: "We went from 'There is asbestos' to 'There isn't asbestos,' to 'There is this,' 'There isn't that,' and the levels of protection changed."

Such information conflicts often were attributed to differences in risk assessment and PPE standards among reporting parties. In other instances, they were attributed to organizational turf battles and personal conflicts. One responder described a safety meeting where specialists from different agencies at the front

For many conference participants, a lack of information on hazards was not a problem. Rather, many spoke of difficulties trying to manage and make sense of a surplus of information. The following statements were made in four different panels:

—There was an eight o'clock safety meeting every morning. There was a nine o'clock contractor meeting every morning. Then there was an afternoon safety meeting and an evening contractor meeting. Then there was the six o'clock meeting at Pier 92. And, on top of all of that, the Fire Department and Police Department had an operational meeting every morning at seven o'clock, at a location that was completely different than where the other two meetings were going on. So it would be hard to get any work done with all the meetings. Eventually, everybody realized what was going on and said, "Okay, we have to try to put it all together," and they did. But it did get a little out of hand at first.

—[Information] would change day to day. We ended up hiring a temp . . . to do nothing but monitor all the different sites from DoD to IAFF to IAFC, CDC, NIOSH. I gave them a list of web sites and I said, "You just [put] these in a circular and you keep giving them to me so I can try and keep up with what the hell everybody's saying."

—You had a lot of entities that had their own specific mission, whether it was the EPA or the military, the FBI, the USAR teams. They all had their own unique perspective of what constituted a hazard, and what was a significant concern to them may not be a concern to another group. They all had good intentions of putting forth their information, but at times it became unnecessarily complicated. We would have crews that would go in at a certain level of protection, working right next to crews that were in an entirely different level of protection. There were questions about which one was right.

—The thing that drives me crazy, and I hate to say it, but all the experts have got to come up with a common theme. I can't have [one federal agency] telling me, "You need Level A protection for this," and [another agency] telling me that a half-faced respirator and latex gloves are sufficient.

of the room began arguing with one another, and as a result, the meeting did not resolve anything.

Some responders who received information on hazards that was not consistent with their personal observations stopped trusting all the information they received from monitoring organizations. "One of the first [reports] . . . said that all of the stuff at the World Trade Center was within normal limits. Now, a lot of that is how you deliver that message, because there was nothing normal about the stuff," said an EMS responder.

Especially in the case of anthrax, keeping up with changing information being provided by numerous agencies was a serious challenge for front-line responder organizations. The desire to have accurate information was of particular concern to commanders, who were making decisions about what level of risk their personnel would face. "You've got to understand what you're dealing with," said a law-enforcement representative. "We can equip our first responders to a certain level . . . but as managers, we have to understand what risks they are capable of dealing with or what hazards [are out there], and we have to weigh what roles they can play." Another said, "If we put them in the wrong outfit and something happens to them, then we're going to get sued. I'm going to get sued personally, perhaps."

Finally, an EMS panel member observed that post-event information can be just as important: Sometimes responders were not told whether the test on the suspicious substance they responded to turned out to be positive for anthrax or not. The responder assumed that they would have been informed if it was positive, but the lack of certainty caused stress anyway.

PERSONAL PROTECTIVE EQUIPMENT INFORMATION AND TRAINING

Pre-Event Information and Training

Emergency responders acknowledged that they receive a large amount of pre-event training regarding PPE and practices. Nevertheless, some firefighters said that initial training as a rookie combined with regular in-service training still left gaps in knowledge. Along the same lines, law-enforcement representatives reported that hand-signal classes are given once a year, but that these classes were not sufficient for their personnel to actually learn and remember the different signals.

According to law-enforcement panelists, personal protective equipment training varies greatly in their community. A Special Weapons and Tactics (SWAT) team may receive 40 hours of hazmat training, while patrol officers receive

> Hopefully the people that are there are professionals who already had training—the HAZWOPER training—and [using PPE] should have been addressed already. But if they're not assigned PPE and trained in them and they don't operate with them, then it becomes an issue on the scene. When you get training on the scene, it's half-assed at best.
>
> *—Firefighter-special-operations panel member*

none. Some agencies use tabletop exercises and scenarios to demonstrate possible hazards, risks, and PPE needs at a scene. A limited amount of training is done using instructional videos. Some of the federal law-enforcement officials present felt that they did receive the proper training. In sum, though, all members of the panel agreed that law enforcement is "behind the curve," compared with other emergency responders, in terms of receiving PPE training or information.

In any case, the consensus among several panels was that unless practices are ingrained before a major incident and the use of equipment and procedures is part of preparedness, responders are unlikely to absorb training fully in the heat of the battle to save lives or to be predisposed to wear personal protective equipment as prescribed. An EMS panelist reiterated this view: "We've had training . . . and then all of a sudden when it starts happening to you, you're going, 'Oh crap, what does my book say?'" The responders did not pay close attention to the material, because it was something they thought they would never see.

On-Site Information and Training

Information and training regarding PPE available at the site was cited in many panels as particularly lacking, especially for personnel not used to working under such conditions.

> Half the time I was wearing the damn things I was still smelling and breathing everything that was going on. They just showed up in cases. I liked the red one, the red one looked better than the black one, so I put the red one on. It fit all right and I wore it. I have no idea to this day what the hell it was.
>
> *—Emergency-medical-services panel member*

Much of the equipment being passed out was unfamiliar to responders, and they had no way to quickly and effectively evaluate which equipment, especially respirators, was appropriate for the task they were doing. Commenting about air-purifying respirators, one special-operations representative said, "You may not know [if] you are in the proper mask. The cartridges are specific for specific things and . . . you've got a million cartridges on site and a million different people giving their ideas." The decision about what respirator to use was often made on the basis of comfort or relatively arbitrary considerations such as appearance, rather than on the basis of solid information, said members of the firefighter and EMS panels. "I was near 25 firefighters who said they didn't want to wear their respirators because of the pink cartridges," reported a health-and-safety panelist.

For the construction-trades personnel, training posed a major challenge, especially given the large numbers of these workers involved in the World Trade Center response.[1] Construction workers lacked PPE training common among firefighters and emergency medical personnel. For example, construction workers typically do not wear respirators. Thus, they were unfamiliar with how to fit them, what filters were required for which situation, and how often canisters needed replacement. Nor were they familiar with the nature of many hazards present on-site. As one panel member put it, "They thought if they couldn't see it or smell it, it couldn't hurt them."

Federal and state agency panelists at the conference disagreed on the thoroughness and effectiveness of on-site respirator training:

—They didn't give out respirators without informing [the users]. I know this. They did not give out a respirator without informing the person they gave it to that the filter should be changed, and they talk about constant use and exposure, and the time limits that you change them. . . . They were trained.

—People are given respirators and not instructed that periodically you have to change cartridges. I saw people taking cartridges off that I don't know how they were getting any air. The initial particulate filter, the outside part of the cartridge, was so black and dirty. Either nobody told them they had to change cartridges out once and a while, or for one reason or another, they'd worn them out and they couldn't find cartridges so they kept what they had.

Several on-site training programs were set up to instruct responders on how to fit and wear respirators. Some testing went on to ensure proper fit. In the trades panel discussion, it was noted that some of these tests were quite simple: An individual can do the positive and negative pressure test by simply blocking the filters and breathing in and out. Other tests are more complicated and require a second party to expose the individual wearing the respirator to a dis-

[1] A large number of trades workers also were employed at the Fresh Kills landfill, the area serving as the repository for debris removed from the World Trade Center, which is being treated as a hazardous-waste site. Fresh Kills had a controlled perimeter, and workers wore protective garments and respirators.

tinctive odor. Thorough fit-testing is even more elaborate. A firefighter complained that guidance on replacing respirator cartridges was not sufficient: "The Health Department said when you feel resistance. Well, hell, we are not going to feel resistance."

Commenting on the pieces of training material that were passed out to workers on-site, panel members stressed that these need to be prepared with the audience and environment in mind. For example, a pamphlet giving instructions on eye safety read in part, "Use ANS1287.1 certified industrial eye protection with 287 on frame." Instructions of this nature are not useful to construction workers on-site. Similarly, law-enforcement panelists suggested labeling packaging or pieces of equipment in simple terminology stating what the equipment will protect against. As they pointed out, during an emergency, no one wants to or is willing to spare the time to look at a reference manual to determine which PPE to use.

Shortcomings in on-site information and training led to some hazardous behavior. For example, construction workers would wear an air-purifying respirator while laboring on the rubble pile but would move only yards away and take it off to eat lunch. They thus were subject to the very hazard the APR was designed to protect them from, as they sat in the same environment breathing the contaminated air and eating food contaminated with the ubiquitous particulate matter. Furthermore, the respirator mask left dangling around one's neck filled with the same particulate, which the worker then inhaled when he put the respirator on and went back to work. Another panelist told of hard hats being worn backwards. Though he was unsure of the reason for this, he pointed out that wearers were probably not aware that this renders the hat less effective and that such behavior could have been prevented through proper training on its use.

The situation with anthrax was more severe. Health-and-safety panel members felt that preparedness for and information and training support during the anthrax attacks were inadequate on all fronts: The response protocols were being developed during the actual responses. One federal-and-state-agency representative noted that while NIOSH had ample information available on what PPE to recommend for silica and asbestos, the agency could offer no help for anthrax, even after several incidents had occurred. They also commented on a perceived tension between public health and occupational safety paradigms for responding to these incidents: The public-health model centers on infectious-disease control and medicating people, while the occupational-safety model treats anthrax like a hazardous material. But one panelist countered, "The essential paradigm for anthrax response nationally has been, If you know hazmat, you know biological. And that is simply not true."

Chapter Five

SITE MANAGEMENT FOR PERSONAL PROTECTION

For many participants, management issues were equally, if not more, important than equipment concerns to the personal protection of emergency responders and others at terrorist-incident sites. Such issues included establishing effective management structures and practices on-site, risk assessment and communications, and PPE enforcement. This chapter reviews key management tasks and functions emergency responders carried out—both in the initial response and during sustained campaigns—at the terrorist-attack sites, as they relate to health and safety and personal protective equipment.

COMMANDING AUTHORITY

A continuing refrain throughout the conference was the need to rapidly establish a single controlling authority or unified command. A smooth and expeditious transition from initial chaotic response characterized by independent service commands to a coordinated incident command with either a single commander or a unified command structure was seen as desirable. Health and safety officials, as well as special-operations personnel, lamented the lack of a unified authority and command structure at the World Trade Center site, a situation initially caused by the loss of key leaders during the building collapse, but one that persisted for several months after the terrorist attack. The absence of an overall authority had important implications for responder health and safety.

Health and safety officials said that the lack of a clear command structure at the World Trade Center thwarted efforts to enforce PPE use and risk-reduction behaviors. A host of organizations from the federal, state, and local level, as well as the private sector, had representatives either permanently or periodically on site. Panelists reported that the PPE standards and procedures they were supposed to follow varied widely. Some organizations had no standards or procedures at all. After the initial response, for example, the City of New York partitioned the site and hired four contractors to remove debris. Each contractor was subject to U.S. Occupational Safety and Health Administration (OSHA) rules, faced the possibility of worker's compensation claims, and was responsible for its own workforce. However, contractor policy on PPE varied, and as a result, employees working next to each other were wearing different levels of protection.

At the Pentagon, inner and outer perimeters were established early on, and a clear command structure made enforcement of PPE more straightforward. Attendees cited similar successes at the Murrah Federal Building in Oklahoma City. A firefighter summed up the situation in Oklahoma City: "You didn't have to wear personal protective equipment, but if you didn't wear PPE, you didn't work on site."

> I guess it was about day three or four that [a person at the Pentagon response] actually put together a safety team briefing, because everybody had their own safety officer, if you will. USAR had theirs, we had ours, FBI had theirs, Army had theirs. So we finally put together a unified command of safety officers who met once every 12-hour block to bring back all the information and decide what was going to be appropriate safety precautions, gear, etc. . . . If you were operating here, it was going to be this. We came up with what the appropriate [PPE] level was, what filter would we wear in our filter masks. Not just the first one that you come across, but which level of filtration will be correct.
>
> —*Firefighter-special-operations panel member*

Finally, there was a consensus among health and safety specialists that a unified and clear chain of command helped address information-flow issues. The absence of such an authority at the World Trade Center made coherent information gathering and dissemination difficult and hindered the specialists' ability to assess and report hazards. A high-level, unified command at the Pentagon was seen as improving health and safety specialists' access to key decisionmakers on site, a key communication issue. Related to this, clearer site control helped to coordinate information provided to site workers and the media and enhanced its credibility.

INCIDENT DEFINITION

Incident definition and transition is another complex management-policy challenge. One health and safety panel member said, "The biggest problem is, when does a situation go from a routine fire where the fire department is in control to become a disaster? When does authority change?" This issue has major implications for PPE requirements, since different kinds of equipment will be called for at a fire site than at a biohazard or chemical hazard site.

> [It's] what we call in the fire service a "continuing size up." What's your initial problem? Plane into the building. Second problem? Fire. You've got people involved in both cases. . . . So you're operating in a fire mode as you gather more information, as you determine, "Hey, the second plane hits, maybe I'm dealing with a terrorist event."
>
> —*Firefighter-special-operations panel member*

At some point, site operations transition from rescue to recovery. This has important ramifications for other aspects of site control, such as PPE supply and enforcement. Defining that point can be both politically difficult and emotional. Views expressed by several special-operations and federal-and-state-agency panel members suggested that officials' realization that there would be a long, sustained campaign at the World Trade Center site came slowly. Within a few days, most believed that no one was going to be found alive in the rubble. Nevertheless, the improvisational approach to PPE use and supervision characteristic of the initial, "urgent" phase of the response (characterized by the principle "risk a life to save a life") was allowed to go on far too long, in the view of these panelists. This resulted in unnecessary risks being taken.

Conversely, as time passes, some hazards also decline. For example, as noted by members of the trades panel, the dust at the World Trade Center began to settle, and people did not require as high a level of breathing protection as they did initially. However, scaling back the level of protection and ensuring that everyone at the site receives accurate information as conditions change is a perpetual challenge. Again, a central site authority can facilitate this process. This issue is not minor, because emergency procedures to save a life may justify accepting a level of risk that is not warranted in recovering the dead.

SCENE CONTROL

A second recurring refrain was the need for immediate and effective perimeter or scene control. Initially, at the terrorist-attack sites, this consisted of responders personally "holding people back" and isolating the scene. As the response evolved, it was necessary to erect a hard perimeter—in this case, a chain-link fence—to make sure that only essential personnel, operating under the direction of the scene commander, were on-site.

Initially, the World Trade Center site had more than 30 access points. Three months after the attack, the number had been reduced to five. The Pentagon site was secured relatively quickly, largely by means of erecting a fence and establishing entry and exit points. The need for rapid emplacement of a perimeter fence was prompted by lessons learned from the Oklahoma City bombing. It was noted in the plenary sessions of the conference and in the EMS panel that site evacuations occurred in response to concern about a secondary explosive device in Oklahoma City and a second incoming airplane at the Pentagon. These evacuations facilitated rapid site isolation and control: Once everyone evacuated, the command structure was able to set up a perimeter to keep nonessential personnel out.

> In Oklahoma City we had the same problem: Everybody was coming. What saved us was we had the second bomb scare and we evacuated everybody. That allowed the PD to put up a hard perimeter. The National Guard, I think, is the best, because they're not going to do the police officer a favor, they're not going to do the fireman a favor, and once we got our perimeter, you weren't getting in, no matter who you were.
>
> —*Firefighter-special-operations panel member*

Establishment of perimeter control at the sites was determined by several factors. One was location. The World Trade Center and the Murrah Federal Building were located in urban areas, making scene control more difficult. Perimeter control at the Pentagon was much more manageable: The site was easier to isolate because the Pentagon is surrounded by freeways, parking lots, and park land, and the very large building itself formed part of the barrier. Furthermore, the federal, state, and local agencies involved were accustomed to working with each other and had practiced emergency-response drills. Several firefighters agreed: "What made it [effective] was the training that we do all the time with the other jurisdictions, commands, and knowing the people." In addition, at the Pentagon, armed and uniformed military personnel were nearby and available to assist in controlling access relatively early.

Perimeter control facilitated enforcement of PPE standards, training, and decontamination. If the PPE standard was a hard hat and a Tyvek™ overgarment, that standard could be monitored and enforced at the controlled entry points. Persons who were not equipped either donned protection available there or did not enter the site: The use of personal protective equipment became part of the "admission ticket" needed to participate in the Pentagon response.

> By the time the MPs were in place the next morning [September 12], plus Virginia State Police as well as county police, we had pretty good control. Then they ended up getting in a chain-link fence. We actually went to an ID system that was set up. It wasn't that great. But finally, within a period of time, you actually had to show ID. They had a picture ID that they printed for you right there, and somebody had to vouch for you and/or show your ID to get in. But that was days into the process.
>
> —*Firefighter-special-operations panel member*

The need for appropriate credentialing was viewed as another essential aspect of perimeter control. Health and safety officials reported considerable confusion and inconsistency at the World Trade Center over who should be allowed into the site and what constituted credentials. In the early phases of the response, said one representative, occupational-health-and-safety personnel had difficulty getting into the site, while "anyone who showed up in scrubs" was admitted. Another panelist reported, "I couldn't get in with a federal ID, but I could have gotten in with a PD shirt or a bunker coat." In contrast, commanders at the Pentagon made use of federal ID badges to create a credentialing system that went into effect within the first few days of the attack there. Trades panel members indicated that putting site control in the hands of an agency from outside the local area, such as the National Guard, was a good strategy. Using an outside agency increases the potential for uniform enforcement of rules to keep out individuals who are not authorized to be on the site.

Proper credentialing was cited as critical for the management and safe activities of volunteers, off-duty responders, and other interested parties (including the media and VIPs).

INTERNAL PERIMETER CONTROL

Control of the site perimeter is only part of the scene-control task. Some panelists indicated that it is also necessary to establish control within the site, particularly with an eye to identifying zones with different levels of hazard and consequently different PPE requirements. At the World Trade Center, officials attempted to do this by painting a green line to delineate an interior perimeter within which personal protective equipment use was required. But this did not work well, in large part due to poor information dissemination and the lack of a central authority to enforce the boundary lines. "I didn't see no green line," said one emergency medical responder. Ultimately, by requiring special "confined space entry" permits to get to the below-grade-level areas at the World Trade Center site (after significant amounts of rubble had been removed), the New York City Department of Design and Construction was able to enforce specific PPE requirements and track personnel in these areas.

> I think what needs to be established quickly are zones. Everybody that was at Ground Zero didn't need the same respiratory protection [as] somebody that was outlying with just debris, construction, and traffic kinds of issues. . . . Early on, zones need to be firmly established and recognized.
>
> —*Firefighter-special-operations panel member*

The concept of inner and outer perimeters was widely endorsed by health and safety officials as critical to allowing health and safety responders to function effectively.

PERSONAL PROTECTIVE EQUIPMENT ENFORCEMENT

Enforcement of PPE use varied significantly between the initial and sustained response phases. It was widely acknowledged that emergency responders assumed higher risks in the initial stage of their efforts to rescue victims.

> [It's] the nature of fire rescue, of law-enforcement personnel . . . when you're confronted with a situation with the potential loss of life, that you will respond. It's not a second thought, you will respond to do what is necessary to rescue individuals wherever they are. We've violated probably every precautionary measure established by NIOSH, etc., but I think when you're confronted with the realities of life, people are going to do what their instincts tell them, and that's to save lives. They'll think about the consequences secondary.
>
> —*Law-enforcement-panel member*

However, several panelists noted that significant risk-taking behavior became somewhat regularized at the World Trade Center site and continued long after the urgency from which it stemmed had passed. Similarly, over the sustained response campaign, enforcement of PPE use at the World Trade Center was seen as significantly more variable than it was at the Pentagon. For example, federal and state panelists noted that enforcement of PPE regulations at the World Trade Center site was, in some instances during the sustained-response phase, purposely relaxed or waived, because a strict enforcement of rules would have required shutting down the entire response operation. Greater variation in PPE use at that site was also due to the fact that regulatory agencies appear to have focused on helping the responders do their jobs safely rather than on citing them for noncompliance. As one federal-and-state-agency panelist noted, when OSHA representatives first arrived on the scene, they acted in an advisory capacity, making sure that workers "understood how things were changing onsite, and what may need to start happening."

Conference attendees highlighted state and federal agencies as very important for enforcing use of personal protective equipment at incident sites. Vesting PPE enforcement authority in an "independent" organization that is not directly involved in the response itself was seen as positive. Having an independent enforcement authority reduces the potential for interagency conflicts—for example, police (with their unique set of standards for personal protective equipment and practices) trying to enforce measures on the local fire department.

> Twice that I know of, they were going to shut down the World Trade Center site completely because of environmental and health issues. They were really pushing for this. Calmer heads prevailed because, can you imagine the political and social impact of just shutting down the World Trade Center at that period of time early on?
>
> — *Federal-and-state-agency panel member*

At the World Trade Center, Pentagon, and Oklahoma City sites, a host of federal, state, and local-level response organizations sent representatives. Members of these groups follow the rules or standard operating procedures and levels of attention of their parent organizations with respect to personal protective equipment. Over time, a wide variation in PPE use makes enforcement difficult. One picture passed around the trades panel showed four workers next to each other, each wearing a different level of breathing protection: One had an SCBA, one had a half-face respirator with canister filters, one had a dust mask, and one had no breathing protection (however, as one panelist noted, he was wearing a hard hat). Such wide variances in PPE use made enforcement difficult: "He's not wearing it, why should I?" was the attitude among many, said a trades panel member. In addition to variation by organization, special-operations personnel noted, PPE enforcement varied by shift supervisor and from squad to squad.

Several instances of variation in PPE enforcement at the World Trade Center were noted in the panel discussions. Protection from falls was available at the site in the form of harnesses and ropes, but according to members of the trades panel, its use was spotty. The equipment takes time to install, and, initially at least, personnel were loath to delay rescue efforts to install it. Another issue was the use of cranes with personnel baskets to lift and position workers. While the practice is common elsewhere, workers at conventional construction sites in New York City are not permitted to use personnel baskets. As a result, they were unfamiliar with the stringent safety procedures required.[1]

Similarly, visibility-enhancing garments, which were available at the World Trade Center site, were not universally worn, in spite of the fact that the hazard of being struck by a vehicle or piece of equipment was relatively high. Once the debris-removal effort progressed from the initial bucket brigade, the site had a large number of vehicles moving around it, from Gators (small, wheeled utility

---

[1]An occupant in a personnel basket should be secured by a harness with the ropes attached above the ball on the crane cable, but apparently this rarely occurred at the World Trade Center site.

vehicles) to heavy construction equipment. The site operated 24 hours a day, and the dust hampered visibility. The personal protective equipment that was available worked well enough, and supplies were ample. Information and enforcement were the issues.

> It's a timeliness issue. Are we saving a person's life now or going to get the equipment to put on first? What wins? The person does. It's as simple as that.
>
> *—Law-enforcement panel member*

Beyond enforcement, a principal determinant of PPE use, according to a consensus among firefighters, was whether it was interfering with their job. A case in point was Personal Alert Safety Systems (PASS), which, among other functions, sense if the wearer has stopped moving for a significant interval. The large number of false alarms at the World Trade Center motivated most firefighters to turn them off or leave them behind. "People won't turn them on because of the nuisance alarms," declared a special-operations panelist. Several other panelists pointed out that the weather was relatively mild during the responses to the terrorist events. If the weather had been hot or cold or rainy, PPE performance and use could have been much worse. Clearly, perceiving hazards also provides an incentive for workers to wear PPE. After an article appeared in a local newspaper discussing the threat posed by asbestos fibers used in a portion of the construction at the World Trade Center, respirator use increased dramatically. Finally, positive incentives can also boost PPE use. A trades panel member noted that PPE tended to be worn at the World Trade Center site if it were somehow related to the incident. As one member put it, "Anything with a flag on it got worn."

Chapter Six

RECOMMENDATIONS FOR MOVING FORWARD

After they had discussed PPE performance, information and training, and site-management issues, conference participants were asked to put forward concrete recommendations about technologies and procedures that could help protect the health and safety of emergency workers as they respond to acts of terrorism. These recommendations, combined with other themes that arose during the panel sessions and plenary presentations, form the basis for the following discussion.

It should be noted that conference participants sometimes disagreed on the merits of certain recommendations, such as the need to develop more broad-spectrum PPE and the need for more PPE training. Also, participants indicated that many of the recommendations they put forth (and the debates about them) have been aired in the past. The terrorist attacks, however, added new force to management and policy discussions.

The recommendations of the conference participants are organized into four areas: (1) the equipment itself; (2) logistical issues affecting PPE; (3) training and information; and (4) management of the disaster site. Management was included because, as panelists suggested, it can have as great an effect on availability and use of PPE as do the other factors. This discussion of conference recommendations is not exhaustive; it is intended to highlight leading themes and to illustrate the PPE issues that front-line responders care most strongly about.

PERSONAL PROTECTIVE EQUIPMENT

Personal protective equipment is designed to protect its users from the health and safety threats they face in the course of their work. Beyond that, the equipment must be practical enough in its design and the demands it places on its users to make it possible for them to do their jobs effectively on a day-to-day basis.

Responders to the terrorist incidents generally argued that they were pleased with the performance of their personal protective equipment when it was employed as intended and for the hazards it was designed to protect against. However, discussants also indicated that many types of currently available PPE have substantial shortcomings in both protection and practicality for situations having the severity and the wide range of hazards that exist at terrorist-attack sites, particularly at the World Trade Center site, and for responding to anthrax incidents. Furthermore, the attendees cautioned that, because of this complex operating environment, an important tradeoff exists between protection and practicality of PPE.

For current technologies, the more completely a piece of gear protects against all of the threats responders face, the more it may restrict their ability to do what they need to do during their regular tasks as well as during these demanding and extended responses. Not surprisingly, panelists sometimes disagreed on the desired balance between protective performance and responder performance. For example, firefighters cautioned that they did not want to see PPE design changes that would make their gear more difficult to use in conventional day-to-day operations.

Hazard Monitoring and Equipment Selection

The panelists, representing a range of responder functions and professions, expressed frustration that using much of today's protective equipment requires extensive knowledge about the particular hazards that exist in the environment. This detailed information is needed because most equipment, whether it is turnout gear optimized for thermal protection or a respirator cartridge for a particular airborne threat, addresses only one or a small range of hazards. With such "narrow-spectrum" PPE, appropriate selection of a respirator cartridge, for example, requires the responder to know what materials in the air must be filtered out. Many participants called for better methods for assessing hazards at a site and, most important, ways to get the information to responders as early in the response as possible. Many responders indicated that the best way this could be addressed was by developing better, faster, and more accurate monitoring technologies that would enable responders to evaluate their working environments for themselves. These technologies include not only better and cheaper monitors for chemical and biological agents but also detectors for more common threats such as volatile organic compounds, particulates, and other environmental hazards.

Panelists emphasized that it is very important that detection and monitoring technologies and practices present their information in a way that is meaningful to the responder. The feeling of one EMS panelist was that most responders would be more interested in tests that indicated what PPE to wear, rather than providing information on the hazard itself. In the absence of tests that provide ready access to information, several panelists indicated that "quick reference cards" for matching up PPE with a best guess about the hazards present could be useful.

Concomitantly, responders called for greater interagency coordination and consistency in their protocols for both hazard identification and PPE selection. Federal-and-state-agency panelists, for example, called for universal classification of PPE according to "type and kind," so that equipment made by different manufacturers and used across different agencies would be subject to a consistent set of functionality definitions and standards.

Another strategy to ameliorate information requirements would be to develop broader-spectrum equipment that would protect against a wider range of threats. Participants favored this strategy particularly for respiratory protection, where the broad range of choices of different types of canisters makes it difficult to know how to select proper protection. A universal respirator cartridge, it was argued, could greatly increase overall protection of the responder community, even if it were not as effective as specialized cartridges, because any responder using one would know that he or she was at least minimally protected against a variety of exposures.

> Remember the balance between protection and usability. Don't design something that is perfectly the maximum safety [but] that is so heavy and so uncomfortable nobody will wear it, because then they really have zero protection.
>
> —*Firefighter panel member*

Some responders cautioned, however, that a move toward more broad-spectrum PPE could be a double-edged sword. As a single piece of protective equipment becomes more and more protective, it often becomes heavier and more bulky, and it limits mobility. For example, a USAR team member indicated that he would appreciate a suit that protected him fully against chemical, biological, physical, and other threats, but it had to be about the same weight and flexibility as the military fatigues he currently wore. Making PPE more cumbersome has the potential negative consequence of the equipment interfering with the emergency responders' primary task, to the point where they choose not to use it. The terrorist incidents demonstrated that responders are willing to discard protective equipment when they believe it impedes their ability to do their jobs. As a consequence, panelists pointed out, practicality must be the overriding concern in future PPE design.

> You've got to go get the bad guys. . . . How do you see? What's your range of vision? Aiming a weapon, putting handcuffs on, wrestling subjects to the ground. I can't be wearing stuff that's all bulked up and restricts my movement when I have those kinds of law-enforcement missions in mind.
>
> —*Law-enforcement panel member*

Given such considerations, other recommendations were made for equipment that provides an intermediate level of protection against a range of threats but has the weight and flexibility that responders need. A special-operations panelist expressed a desire for a BDU with "some chemical, some biological, and better waterproofing characteristics" that would enable responders to operate better in multihazard environments and could more easily be decontaminated at the end of the day. Several special-operations and EMS panelists recommended that to provide more flexibility, their organizations could adopt several different levels of PPE (also termed *scenario-based PPE*) geared toward different hazards—a strategy developed for hazmat operations. Finally, panelists asked for easy-to-use compatibility charts to guide the use of the different levels of PPE, as is done for hazmat operations.

> *In an effort to simplify PPE decisionmaking and allow personnel to better match equipment to hazards in the absence of certain information, the EMS panel proposed a three-level, task-specific model for PPE use. Such an approach is similar to the way equipment is allocated on hazardous-materials teams, and similar "levels-based" approaches were suggested by other meeting attendees.*
>
> *Level A* is the highest threat/greatest protection, for a fire/rescue situation. This would include SCBA, turnout coat and pants, boots, gloves, and a heavy helmet.
>
> *Level B* would be for an intermediate threat, such as rescue in a non-fire environment. It would be lighter because it wouldn't have to protect against extremely high temperatures. It would include some sort of coveralls, an APR, and a lighter helmet.
>
> *Level C* would be for a biological threat, consisting primarily of a blood-borne pathogen barrier, biological air-filter mask, and eye shield.
>
> Levels B and C would also include an escape hood with supplied air, suitable to protect the responder for about 15 minutes in a hazardous environment, and hearing protection included on each responder's belt.

Other Recommendations for Equipment Improvements

The importance of respirators in the response to the terrorist attacks led to several recommendations about their design. Respirators that are more comfortable and practical for workers on extended duty at large-scale disaster sites were a clear priority of the participants. Suggestions included exploring full-face models and evaluating how well respirators meet the needs of workers doing strenuous work. Several panels suggested that supplied-air or powered respirators were the preferred choices, since they put less of the burden on the user's lungs. Supplied-air respirators also can be used in an oxygen-deficient environment, and the user does not have to worry about clogging filters. Integration of voice diaphragms or emitters in respirator masks to allow communication was also a clear priority of the participants. Law-enforcement personnel indicated that the stress and activities at the terrorist-attack sites caused some people to overtighten their masks, which led to breakage. Strengthening the materials used in the masks could compensate for that problem. Responders to the anthrax attacks also expressed a particular and specific concern about whether the HEPA filters used on most masks were adequate to protect against military-grade anthrax.

The need for providing escape hoods with supplied air to all emergency responders was seen as an important priority for the EMS panel. One participant commented, "We've almost come to the realization that the first groups that go into something ugly are going to die. None of that's acceptable, but we haven't solved it. Maybe that's the chance of this bailout [technology]. It may solve that problem."

Both firefighters and special-operations personnel noted that their gloves were too bulky for rescue work. They asked for thermal protection in a smaller, thinner glove. It was further recommended that efforts be directed at developing workable eye protection that protected against particulate matter but would not fog up during physical exertion. The firefighter panel uniformly agreed that a lighter helmet that was as effective as the current standard gear would be desirable in extended campaigns. They stressed that any new version, however, should retain the traditional shape.

AVAILABILITY OF PERSONAL PROTECTIVE EQUIPMENT

Supply

The conference presentations and panel discussions revealed numerous key situations in which PPE was not sufficiently available to emergency responders at the major terrorist-attack sites. The attendees clearly believed that more could be done to provide appropriate PPE to responders—those initially responding to the event, those dispatched to the scene during the sustained campaign, and volunteers. A common refrain was that all responders working in the same environment should have access to appropriate protection irrespective of their particular role or organizational affiliation.

During the discussions, it was pointed out that new funding is becoming available to build and replenish prepositioned emergency-response caches, and several recommendations were put forth on this subject:

- Caches (such as those maintained by FEMA) should contain a larger amount of personal protective equipment, so that local responders and supplemental units could be fully equipped and replenished with new gear as needed. Firefighter panelists recommended that caches contain ample supplies of boots, gloves, PAPRs, and lighter-weight clothing, such as coveralls.
- The positioning and staging of the caches should take into account the potential for air-transportation shutdowns or other disruptions in the transportation infrastructure.
- Caches should be managed at different levels—local, regional, and national. This approach would help ensure that a minimum amount of equipment is available nearby for immediate access in an emergency, with additional stores available at the regional and national levels for supporting progressively larger events. Alternatively, incoming FEMA Urban Search and Rescue teams should be prepared to bring in a supply of equipment for local responders who are already on the scene, especially in smaller jurisdictions that might not have sufficient supplies on hand.
- Regulations should be promulgated requiring that the PPE procured (for example, with federal funds) meet certain minimal performance standards: "It must be tested and certified to nationally recognized standards," emphasized one special-operations panelist.
- Those supplying the caches must take into account the fact that emergency responders come in all shapes and sizes, so simply stocking large sizes of garments, gloves, or masks will leave many responders without appropriate gear.
- In light of the number of responders who lacked basic PPE at the attack sites, federal grants for PPE should require that recipient organizations outfit all responders with a basic PPE ensemble before spending any money on expensive, high-tech equipment.

Problems with equipment performance brought up the important role that equipment manufacturers can play in responding to terrorist events. Conference attendees suggested that inventory databases be developed for site commanders, so that they can quickly determine what PPE is available in nearby warehouses and request shipment of the most critical goods. Such a database, federal-and-state-agency panelists noted, could act as a "national shopping list" for emergency responders by identifying and monitoring sources of supply, as well as manufacturing and distribution capabilities. This would improve coordination between manufacturers and emergency-response agencies and would help assure that agencies could locate and acquire the appropriate equipment as quickly as possible. Finally, special-operations panelists went further to say that commanders should have proper information and the authority to turn away offers of equipment that would not be useful.

Interoperability

Even though a large supply of protective equipment, particularly respirators, was shipped to New York City in the wake of the World Trade Center attacks, problems with equipment interoperability caused much of that material to be effectively unavailable to many responders. Participants emphasized that interoperability should be a prime consideration whenever equipment availability and certification was discussed.

Specifically, it was recommended that all federal agencies acquiring and stocking personal protective equipment use identical brands or, at the least, interoperable equipment. Some participants went further and called for federal regulations mandating that equipment purchased by responder organizations meet some standard of interoperability. Another recommendation was that NIOSH or another agency with jurisdiction issue binding regulations establishing standard couplings on respirators so that cartridges and masks could be used interchangeably. Some suggested an interim strategy for smaller emergency-response organizations that are more likely to call on outside assistance: Coordinate PPE acquisitions and logistics with other local and state jurisdictions to ensure interoperability.

> We need an interchangeable battery [for flashlights], just like in a radio. You pop the old battery off and put a new battery on. With a built-in battery, yeah it's great. It's waterproof and all, but it's not serving its purpose when you need to change it right away.
>
> —*Firefighter panel member*

INFORMATION AND TRAINING

Attendees at the conference universally emphasized the importance of knowledge and information. The law-enforcement panel listed knowledge as the *primary* ingredient for successful protection. This included both the knowledge that responders gain through PPE training and the information needed to use the equipment appropriately. Many responders also argued that interagency training is key to effective implementation of health and safety measures and PPE enforcement.

Personal Protective Equipment Training

Many panel members called for more PPE training in advance of terrorist incidents, arguing it is more effective than training provided under the high-pressure conditions of the response itself. They also recommended that equipment needed for these types of major responses be integrated into the standard operating procedures of organizations as much as possible.

Many participants recommended PPE training for the entire range of responders at a large-scale response site. For example, a special-operations panelist argued that construction workers should be given federal HAZWOPER[1] training and certification so that they would be able to choose proper respirators and be able to identify hazards. "Those people need to be focused on," he concluded.

> One of the things that you've got to remember is that when you are actually engaged, that is not the time to pull somebody aside and give them a training course. In the middle of battle you don't have time to be pulling people and saying, "Let's get the slides out and go over the procedures."
>
> *— Federal-and-state-agency panel member*

Trades panel members suggested that developing a way to readily identify who has been trained in what areas would assist with both advance training and on-scene training. The use of photo badges with clearly visible coding (e.g., colored strips) was put forth as one way to provide such identification. One special-operations panelist further suggested that disaster training should be standardized across responder organizations as much as possible to ensure that everyone has a common knowledge base. In the case of private firms, this could involve formal precertification similar to fulfilling the requirements for working on other hazardous-materials sites.

Some participants questioned the effectiveness of existing training approaches and suggested that more training would have a marginal impact. "The best PPE is between your ears. The problem is, we weren't engaging it," said an EMS panel member.

---

[1]Hazardous Waste Operation and Emergency Response training stipulated in Federal Regulation 29CFR 1910.120.

Hazard Information

Providing accurate hazard information to responders as quickly as possible was highlighted as a key issue by almost every responder panel. As noted above, one step toward this goal would be the development and diffusion of improved environmental monitoring technologies. But, as several panels stressed, the ability to disseminate hazard information, particularly across agencies, also needs to be improved. Many panels called for greater coordination among the monitoring divisions and safety units of responding organizations—a sort of unified incident command for worker safety and health—to ensure that data are coordinated, vetted, and disseminated in a way that is useful and credible to front-line responders. Health-and-safety panelists called for a federal effort to standardize environmental monitoring and data-collection technologies and practices. They also suggested logging and tracking on-site environmental monitoring in a geographic information system to make information available to lead authorities.

> We would ask them to interpret [safety information] into plain English for us. Please stop speaking OSHA-speak, please stop speaking EPA-speak. Speak English so we know what to do.
>
> *—Firefighter panel member*

Emergency-Response Training

The need for pre-disaster training came up repeatedly in many panels. Extensive training, particularly among military units, was cited in the discussions as a reason for the comparatively smooth handling of the disaster response and use of PPE at the Pentagon site. Representatives from local and federal agencies also had practiced joint responses—for instance, under the auspices of Northern Virginia Regional Response and the Washington Metropolitan Council of Governments. Such exercises, it was argued, can play a very important role in building relationships that enable managers to deal more expeditiously with the problems that arise in the heat of a real emergency. “In a unified command, if there’s a breakdown, relationships help,” concluded a special-operations panelist. In addition, these kinds of relationships provide responders with the knowledge of other organizations’ capabilities and needs in the event of an emergency. In contrast, an EMS panel member observed that in New York City, the number of multiagency mass-casualty-incident drills had decreased over the past several years.

Panelists also emphasized the importance of being inclusive in pre-disaster training and exercises. Because of the nature of large-scale disaster responses, every type of responder is on the "front lines" and facing similar threats. Cross-training among different responder groups allows information that might traditionally be held in special units within firefighting or law-enforcement organizations to benefit a broader cross-section of the responder community. A member of the special-operations panel argued that since these incidents force line firefighters to take on new roles, they must be trained so that they can fill the new roles safely. Safety and health officials stressed that hospital staffs should also be included in training exercises.

The ability to sustain a long response to a large-scale incident depends on the logistical capabilities that can be put in place. Including the people and organizations responsible for developing and operating logistics systems in the planning discussions can provide them with a better understanding of the needs of responders. Conversely, incident commanders can gain more accurate knowledge and expectations of which logistics capabilities are—and, importantly, are not—likely to be available. EMS and special-operations panelists also indicated that foul-weather disaster training is another urgent need. The response and logistics in Oklahoma City, the Pentagon, and the World Trade Center all benefited from relatively mild weather. The responses would have been very different if the weather had been very hot or very cold, or if it had been snowing.

> We could have had four feet of snow, we could have had temperatures that were below freezing, because we had people sleeping in tents, you had all the volunteers not wearing appropriate [gear] delivering stuff, handing out things. We would have been bottlenecked with traffic; we would have not been able to get the resources in. If I was New York, and likewise Washington, Arlington, I would sit down with the group of commanders and I'd say, "Okay, what happens if this happens in a foul weather environment? How are we going to get our engines and stuff to the scene? What are we going to do?"
>
> *—Emergency-medical-services panel member*

MANAGEMENT

During panel discussions, conference participants consistently made it clear that management practices at incident sites are intimately tied to protecting the health and safety of emergency responders. Panelists returned repeatedly to the need for quick and effective establishment of an effective command authority over an incident site. Until such authority is established, it is difficult to address any of the other concerns about responder protection. The panelists also made clear that the plans made for establishing command over a disaster site must be sufficiently resilient and robust to handle situations that can disrupt them—for example, backup supervisors should be trained to take over in case of the loss of senior personnel. The World Trade Center response was particularly hampered by the loss of much of the key FDNY leadership and the destruction of the city's disaster coordination center, which had been housed in the World Trade Center complex.

Panelists also emphasized the importance of quickly gaining control of the disaster scene itself. Several participants argued that the experience at the Pentagon, which some panelists noted built on lessons learned in Oklahoma City six years earlier, could serve as a model for perimeter control. Though the Pentagon attack site was easier to manage because of its layout, the procedures used—namely, isolate the site and establish entry and exit control under the aegis of a single agency—generalize well to any site of a terrorist attack. The firefighter panel recommended that guidelines be developed advising city managers to immediately hire fencing contractors when a large incident occurs.

Controlling a disaster site is important for a broad range of reasons. In all of the major disaster sites, many individuals converged soon after the event to volunteer their services. In addition to off-duty emergency responders and medical personnel, many other individuals who were not trained or prepared to participate safely in the response came and volunteered. Some panelists believed that the presence of these people was not beneficial. Keeping out individuals who should not be on the scene protects not only their own health and safety, but also that of responders who might have to act to protect the volunteers.

> One of the big issues [at the Pentagon] was that [we] had all these people there on the scene that didn't belong there. We had an impending threat of another plane coming . . . [emergency personnel] are not going to leave the site until they get the civilians and the do-gooders out of the way. Had the other plane come, we would have lost a lot of people, just because we didn't have any control over the area.
>
> —*Emergency-medical-services panel member*

One responder suggested a mandatory staging system where mutual-aid responders gather in a staging area and then are selectively brought to the scene as a way to control the confusion associated with an influx of well-intentioned volunteers. This was also highlighted as being important for other categories of individuals who invariably come to an incident site, such as politicians, other VIPs, and members of the media.

It is also only through rigorous perimeter control that site managers have the opportunity to track who enters and leaves the site. Such tracking is important as a means of accounting for responders who might be become trapped, for example, by being injured falling into a void in rubble. Panelists indicated that strict access control combined with effective personnel-location technologies is the most effective way to account for individuals working in very chaotic and dangerous environments.

> With all of these incidents, you've got everybody coming in and you lose control. And the reality is, you can't use all those people to start with. You have to break tradition. Traditionally, fire departments have had the mentality that, for a big incident, all the neighboring jurisdictions come to help. That goes back to the old volunteer days of the 1700s, 1800s, the bucket brigades. And we just have to realize that on a large-scale incident like this, we can't do it.
>
> *—Emergency-medical-services panel member*

Health-and-safety panelists recommended that bar-coded identification cards linked to personnel records be used to enable agencies to track on-site personnel. Such control would also provide a chance to verify that the individuals entering a site have the training and fit-testing they need to work safely and use protective equipment appropriately. In addition to tracking the people who are on the incident site at any given time, access control also makes it possible to generate records indicating which responders were exposed to particular hazards during their work at the site. Such exposure data are absolutely critical for public-health professionals seeking to understand the health effects associated with a response. Public-health panelists also emphasized that such exposure data can also be used to protect responders by appropriately "cycling out" workers who have been exposed to hazards.

> We have some very clear lessons learned from the role of public health historically, and that is the need to know who your population at risk is. It's inherent in the establishment of a perimeter, although we don't establish that perimeter or control it. But knowing the population at risk, defining their duration of exposure so you can put things in perspective, eventually translates into the ability to do trauma epidemiology, the analysis of which ends up in recommendations that could be applied to improving the quality or the design of PPE.
>
> *—Health-and-safety panel member*

Perimeter control and effective authority at an incident site are also critical for another high-priority request made by responders at the conference: enforcement of PPE use. Numerous responders across a broad range of panels indicated that enforcement of the proper and constant use of personal protective equipment is an absolute necessity at disaster sites. Once perimeters are fixed with defined entry and exit points, appropriate protective equipment can become part of the "admission ticket" that allows workers to enter a site. A number of special-operations responders commented that compliance with PPE requirements was often higher among members of special-operations units because they knew that being caught violating the rules meant they would be sent home. By establishing a secure perimeter around an incident site, commanders who are responsible for the safety and health of their subordinates can make the same threat to their members—either wear the appropriate PPE or be sent outside the site perimeter.

> We can help facilitate it, but the change is going to have to come from the Fire Department, from the Police Department, and from the Emergency Medical Services folks. They are the ones that are going to have to make a conscious decision to outfit their people with protective equipment to deal with this kind of stuff.
>
> *— Federal-and-state-agency panel member*

Opinions on how compliance should be enforced were mixed. Several attendees suggested that it would be best if the role of enforcing the use of PPE were undertaken by an independent organization that could make more objective judgments about the safety of the responders. A number of panels mentioned a stronger role for OSHA in this regard. Yet another view was that if a unified command of responder safety and health organizations were set up to bring together and rationalize the hazard information provided to responders, the enforcement activity could conceivably be a responsibility of the commander of that network of organizations.

> It's great to have the equipment, great to say you're supposed to use it, but it has to be enforced.
>
> *—Firefighter-special-operations panel member*

One sensitivity that conference participants acknowledged is the difficulty of knowing the appropriate time in a response to begin scrupulously enforcing the use of personal protective equipment. It was broadly acknowledged that during the early phases of a response, when there is still a reasonable probability of rescuing people alive, it is appropriate to allow responders to take personal risk because of the potential for other lives to be saved. This is in line with the credo expressed by many responders at the conference, that they will "risk a life to save a life." It was also considered unreasonable to begin rigorously enforcing PPE use before sufficient equipment is available. As one firefighter commented, "It is hard for me to say, [but] once everybody has their gear, if they aren't wearing it, hit the road." Understanding the sensitivity of the issue, federal-and-state-agency panelists nonetheless urged that efforts be made to increase PPE compliance in the initial response. As a step in this direction, one panelist proposed a middle ground wherein simplified alternative options would be designed for personal protection in immediate and urgent situations.

At some point, however, an incident must transition from a rescue to a recovery phase. At that point, when responders are focused on recovering the dead, gathering evidence, or cleaning up the scene, it is no longer appropriate to allow responders to work without adequate protection. Because of the obvious difficulty of making the call that a response has gone from the rescue to the recovery phase, conference attendees again stated that this decision may be best left to organizations and decisionmakers less directly affected by the emotional impact of the incident.

Chapter Seven

CONCLUDING REMARKS

The emergency workers and managers who attended the NIOSH/RAND conference provided a wealth of information on availability, use, performance, and management of personal protective equipment. Throughout the conference, a number of important, strategic policy issues also emerged. Some of these issues were explicitly addressed during the meeting; others are implicit consequences of the lessons learned. This concluding chapter draws out several of these strategic policy issues for further reflection.

GUIDELINES

One of the clear messages of the conference was that most emergency workers do not believe that they are prepared with the necessary information, training, and equipment to cope with many of the challenges associated with the response to a major disaster such as the World Trade Center attack or for threats associated with anthrax and similar agents. These challenges include the large scale of the operations, the long duration of the response, the broad range of known and potential hazards encountered, and the assumption of nonstandard tasks by emergency responders.

Lessons learned from the response to the terrorist attacks suggest that near-term efforts to develop and upgrade equipment and operating guidelines could significantly improve the safety of emergency workers.

- Guidelines are needed for designing personal protective equipment ensembles appropriate for long-term responses to a range of major disasters.[1] An obvious case would be a disaster involving the collapse of one or more large buildings and the consequent need to work on rubble in the presence

[1] By an ensemble, we mean the entire list of PPE responders should carry, including respirators, clothing, eye protection, sensors, etc.

of a variety of hazards, including human remains, smoldering fires, and airborne contaminants derived from the building and its collapse.

- Recognizing that different responders have different personal protection requirements, these guidelines could also address the various professional groups working at a disaster site. Moreover, the guidelines should take into account the reality that individual responders may fulfill various tasks entailing different hazards and that hazards vary within the inner and outer perimeters of a disaster site.
- Protective equipment and safety guidelines could lead to better responses to biological incidents, not only for anthrax but for other potential biological threats.
- Well-designed guidelines and protocols could significantly improve real-time on-site hazard assessments. Essential elements include sensing equipment, measurement sites, organizational responsibilities and authorities, and data interpretation consistent with operational requirements.
- Discussions about the management of the terrorist attack sites often touched (sometimes indirectly) on sensitive and debated topics such as the appropriate time to declare an end to rescue efforts, the way off-duty and volunteer assistance should be managed, and the accommodation of VIPs and other concerned parties. Given the understandable difficulty of making such decisions in the midst of a response effort, site commanders could greatly benefit from guidelines developed in advance of an incident.
- To be useful, guidelines must be practical in the sense that they consider the capabilities of emergency-response organizations, are easy to use in the field, and do not unduly impair the ability of emergency responders to perform critical lifesaving missions.

COST

The conference participants identified many new technologies for personal protection that would be desirable, based on the lessons learned from the terrorist attacks. Some argued that many desired technologies already exist and progress may simply be a question of procuring the appropriate equipment. Participants highlighted, however, that in the case of both existing and new technology, cost can be a very serious barrier to adoption of equipment by state and local response organizations. Powered-air respirators, for example, can cost ten times as much as the simpler nonpowered variety. Providing each emergency worker with his or her own ensemble of equipment specific to a range of hazards could be prohibitively expensive for most local emergency-response organizations.

Efforts could be directed toward making these technologies more affordable or, alternatively, developing efficient ways to deliver the appropriate equipment to incident sites. In instances where a desired technology is commercially available, expanding the number of prepositioned caches of such equipment that could be moved to response sites could be a good compromise solution. The know-how in supply logistics resident in the U.S. military could be helpful for developing supply strategies for the domestic emergency-response community. Another option would be preplanned equipment-sharing with non-neighboring emergency-response units.[2] For smaller departments, it may be appropriate to examine alternative approaches to increasing purchasing power, such as banding together and conducting coordinated procurements.

RESEARCH, DEVELOPMENT, AND TECHNOLOGY TRANSFER

Several panels put forth recommendations for new equipment and technologies, most of which were for modest advances and incremental improvements to existing technologies. Research and development (R&D), however, may yield significant benefits to the emergency-responder community. For example, a major theme that ran through many of the panels was the apparent tradeoff between the level of protection provided by equipment and the discomfort and physical burden the equipment placed upon those using it. Directing R&D toward advanced respirators, clothing, sensors, and other safety gear may be able to reduce that tradeoff. Other areas suggested by the conference discussions include applications of information technology and communications systems for better management of worker safety at disaster sites and continued emphasis on technologies for locating responders buried or trapped under rubble.

As previously discussed, a theme that arose in several panel discussions was that the purchasing power of the emergency-response community was limited, given its relatively small size and tight budgets, especially at the local level. These factors constrain the community's ability to drive R&D on new technologies. However, much of the safety-related technology that is in use came through technology transfer from other industries, and in some cases, the military. Technology transfer is expected to continue to play an important role in providing emergency responders with improved safety equipment, for example, equipment using information technology, telecommunications, and advanced sensor systems originally developed for purposes other than emergency response.

---

[2]In the event of a major disaster, neighboring emergency-response organizations are likely to be part of the response team and unavailable to share equipment.

Technology transfer can help reduce personal protective equipment costs by spreading R&D outlays across a larger user community. It can also speed the introduction of new technologies to the emergency-response community. But the emergency-response community also has special safety needs that may not be adequately met through technology transfer alone. Many at the meeting suggested that publicly supported R&D would be appropriate for addressing the safety needs of emergency responders. The recent terrorist attacks have raised awareness of this issue.

EQUIPMENT STANDARDIZATION AND INTEROPERABILITY

Equipment standardization and interoperability, as well as the development of more uniform training, maintenance, and use protocols, were mentioned as important needs throughout the conference discussions. Although these are not new issues, the scale and complexity of the terrorist attacks and the problems encountered in the responses appear to have drawn greater attention to them and have increased their importance as policy matters for all members of the emergency-response community. The recommendations put forth by conference participants indicate that these issues may be addressed from the top down (through the promulgation of uniform federal standards) or from the bottom up (through greater interagency cooperation).

SAFETY MANAGEMENT

One of the most important lessons learned from the responders at the terrorist-attack sites is the importance of on-site safety management. Effective safety management is unlikely to be achieved if the overall site is not under a defined management structure, with clear lines of authority and responsibility. The operational side of safety management involves hazard monitoring and assessment, safety-equipment logistics and maintenance, site access control, health and safety monitoring, and medical treatment of emergency workers.

Given the magnitude of these tasks, conference participants argued that the safety officer at a disaster site should be an independent official whose sole responsibility is safety enforcement. In cases where incident sites are managed through a unified command structure, those responsible for responder safety could be part of that command.

From the federal perspective, an important issue is reassessing and clearly defining the roles and relationships of various federal agencies with health and safety responsibilities at a major disaster site.

ORGANIZING PARTNERS

CONFERENCE SPONSOR

National Institute for Occupational Safety and Health

CONFERENCE ORGANIZATION AND MANAGEMENT

RAND Science and Technology Policy Institute

ORGANIZING PARTNERS

Fire Department of New York

InterAgency Board for Equipment Standardization and InterOperability

International Association of Fire Chiefs

International Association of Fire Fighters

National Institute of Justice

National Institute of Standards and Technology

National Fire Protection Association

Oklahoma City National Memorial Institute for the Prevention of Terrorism

U.S. Army Soldier and Biological Chemical Command

U.S. Department of Defense

White House Office of Science and Technology Policy

Appendix B

CONFERENCE PARTICIPANTS

Cynthia Aaron
Department of Emergency Medicine, University of Massachusetts Memorial Medical Center; American College of Medical Toxicology

James Angerett
Fort Myer Fire Department

Ed Bailor
U.S. Capitol Police

Stanley Baldwin
New York City Department of Environmental Protection

Roger Barker
Center for Research Textile Protection & Comfort, North Carolina State University

Steve Beaumont
Washington State Urban Search and Rescue

John Becker
Occupational Health & Environmental Safety, 3M Company

Paul Bennett
New York City Department of Environmental Protection

Samuel Benson
New York City Office of Emergency Management

Bruce P. Bernard
Medical Section, National Institute for Occupational Safety and Health, U.S. Centers for Disease Control and Prevention

Sandra Berrios-Torres
National Center for Injury Prevention and Control, U.S. Centers for Disease Control and Prevention

Roland BerryAnn
Policy Development Team, National Institute for Occupational Safety and Health, U.S. Centers for Disease Control and Prevention

James Blocker
Emergency Medical Services, Oklahoma City Fire Department

Fred Blosser
National Institute for Occupational Safety and Health, U.S. Centers for Disease Control and Prevention

Edward Blunt
Arlington Professional Fire Fighters Association, IAFF Local 2800; Arlington County Fire Department

Richard W. Braddee
National Institute for Occupational Safety and Health, U.S. Centers for Disease Control and Prevention

Robert P. Browne
New York City Fire Department

Craig Buckley
Fairfax County Fire and Rescue

Ronald C. Burger
National Center for Environmental Health, U.S. Centers for Disease Control and Prevention

Stewart Burkhammer
Bechtel Group, Inc.

Todd Carroll
Kappler Safety Group

Don Carson
Training Center, International Union of Operating Engineers

Kimberly Chapman
U.S. Coast Guard

Allen Cherson
New York City Fire Department

Joseph Chiafari
Safety Command, New York City Fire Department

John Clair
New York City Fire Department

Lee Clarke
Safety and Health Department, American Federation of State, County, and Municipal Employees

Stephen Clendenin
Hazmat Response, Massachusetts Urban Search and Rescue

Ron Cobos
Arizona Urban Search and Rescue

David Collins
Turner Construction

Janice Comer Bradley
International Safety Equipment Association

Dean W. Cox
Fairfax County Fire and Rescue Department

Laurie Cummings
U.S. Army Center for Health Promotion & Preventive Medicine, U.S. Army

Wayne Davis
Nuclear, Biological and Chemical Defense Systems, Army Soldier, Biological, Chemical Command, U.S. Army

Melburn Dayton
U.S. Coast Guard

Tim Dowd
Bechtel Group, Inc.

John M. Dower
National Institute for Occupational Safety and Health, U.S. Centers for Disease Control and Prevention

Richard Duffy
International Association of Fire Fighters

Jeff Dyar
U.S. Federal Emergency Management Agency

James Earl
New York City Fire Department

Tom Eggleston
MIZT, MAPA Professional

Kenneth Ellerbe
District of Columbia Fire and Emergency Medical Services

David Evans
National Institute of Standards and Technology

John Eversole
International Association of Fire Chiefs

Michael J. Fagel
North Aurora (Illinois) Emergency Management Agency; North Aurora Fire Department

Tom Fargione
Albany County Sheriff's Department, New York State Emergency Management Office

Frank Fazzio
New York State Department of Labor

George-Wesley Fisher
Defense Protective Service, U.S. Department of Defense

Mark Flomenbaum
New York City Medical Examiner's Office

Stephen Foley
National Fire Protection Association

Caroline Freeman
U.S. Occupational Safety and Health Administration

Bob Garvey
Federal/State Operations, U.S. Occupational Safety and Health Administration

Jim Gass
Oklahoma City Memorial Institute for the Prevention of Terrorism

Tim Gerhart
IAFF Local 36; District of Columbia Fire and Emergency Medical Services

Matt Gillen
National Institute for Occupational Safety and Health, U.S. Centers for Disease Control and Prevention

Zachary Goldfarb
Emergency Medical Services, New York City Fire Department

Richard Goldstein
Uniformed Fire Officers, IAFF Local 854; New York City Fire Department

Sam Gonzales
Oklahoma City Police Department

John Graham
District Council of Carpenters

Danny Gray
Fairfax County Professional Fire Fighters and Paramedics, IAFF Local 2068; Fairfax County Fire & Rescue

Wilbur Gray
Arlington County Fire Department

Jane Greenko
New York City Department of Health

Marie Haring-Sweeney
National Institute for Occupational Safety and Health, U.S. Centers for Disease Control and Prevention

Bill Haskell
Natick Soldier Center, Army Soldier, Biological, Chemical Command, U.S. Army

Bryan Heirston
Oklahoma City Fire Department

Ron Herring
Mine Safety Appliances

Daniel John Hewett
National Institute for Occupational Safety and Health, U.S. Centers for Disease Control and Prevention

Ed Hill
Oklahoma City Police Department

Thomas Hodous
National Institute for Occupational Safety and Health, U.S. Centers for Disease Control and Prevention

Brian Houghton
Oklahoma City Memorial Institute for the Prevention of Terrorism

Joseph T. Hughes, Jr.
National Institute of Environmental Health Sciences

Robert Ingram
Hazmat Operations, New York City Fire Department

Stephen Jarvela
U.S. Environmental Protection Agency

Kenneth Johnson
Arlington County Fire Department

Kerry Kelly
New York City Fire Department

Richard Kelly
Oklahoma City Professional Fire Fighters, Local 157; Oklahoma City Fire Department

John Kimball
Federal Emergency Management Agency

Arthur Lakiotes
New York City Fire Department

John Lambkin
New York City Police Department

Howard Leadbetter
U.S. Federal Bureau of Investigation

Steven Lenhart
National Institute for Occupational Safety and Health, U.S. Centers for Disease Control and Prevention

Andy Levinson
International Association of Fire Fighters

Troy Lipp
Maryland Urban Search and Rescue

Bruce Lippy
National Hazmat Program, International Union of Operating Engineers

Walt Loftus
3M Company

Max Lum
National Institute for Occupational Safety and Health, U.S. Centers for Disease Control and Prevention

Arthur Lynch
U.S. Postal Inspection Service

Raymond Lynch
New York City Mayor's Office of Emergency Management

George Lyon
Arlington County Fire Department

Tom Manley
Uniformed Firefighters Association, IAFF Local 94; New York City Fire Department

Dino Mattorano
National Institute for Occupational Safety and Health, U.S. Centers for Disease Control and Prevention

Philip Mattson
National Institute of Standards and Technology

Phil McArdle
Uniformed Firefighters Association, IAFF Local 94; New York City Fire Department

Davitt McAteer
International Union of Operating Engineers

George McDonald
Transportation Workers of America

Jack McDonald
Uniformed Fire Officers, IAFF Local 854; New York City Fire Department

William Scott McKay
Arlington County Professional Fire Fighters, IAFF Local 2800; Arlington County Fire Department

Kelly McKinney
New York City Department of Health

Mary Merced
Emergency Medical Services, New York City Fire Department

Richard Metzler
National Institute for Occupational Safety and Health, U.S. Centers for Disease Control and Prevention

Jim Miller
New York City Department of Health

Michael Miller
U.S. Army Corps of Engineers

Izzy Miranda
Safety and Health Department, American Federation of State, County, and Municipal Employees

Ray Montero
U.S. Postal Inspection Service

John Moran
National Institute of Environmental Health Sciences

D'arcy Morgan
National Institute of Justice

Craig Moultan
U.S. Occupational Safety and Health Administration

Peter Nacci
National Institute of Justice

Rita Nardella
New York City Mayor's Office of Emergency Management

R. Douglas Nester
U.S. Army Corps of Engineers

Daniel Nigro
New York City Fire Department

Neil Norrell
Response and Prevention Branch, Environmental Protection Agency

Andrea Okun
National Institute for Occupational Safety and Health, U.S. Centers for Disease Control and Prevention

Michael Pagano
Mason Tenders Training, Mason Tenders Council

Kara R. Perritt
National Institute for Occupational Safety and Health, U.S. Centers for Disease Control and Prevention

Mark Persutti
Naval Safety Center

Robert L. Petrone
Bioterrorism Preparedness and Response, Oklahoma State Department of Health

John Pine
IAFF Local F-253; Ft. Myer Fire Department

Tom Pope
U.S. Occupational Safety and Health Administration

Jefferson Prather
Directorate of Deployment Health, U.S. Department of Defense

Dr. David Prezant
New York City Fire Department

Lloyd Randall
Arizona Urban Search & Rescue

Kathleen M. Rest
National Institute for Occupational Safety and Health, U.S. Centers for Disease Control and Prevention

Neal Richmond
New York City Fire Department

Donald Rothchild
Uniformed Emergency Medical Services, New York City Fire Department

H. Kenneth Sacks
National Institute for Occupational Safety and Health, U.S. Centers for Disease Control and Prevention

Michael Sellitto
Special Operations, District of Columbia Fire and Emergency Medical Services

Dan Shipp
International Safety Equipment Association

Louis D. Smith
National Institute for Occupational Safety and Health, U.S. Centers for Disease Control and Prevention

Carol Merry Stephenson
National Institute for Occupational Safety and Health, U.S. Centers for Disease Control and Prevention

Elaine Stewart-Craig
Army Soldier, Biological, Chemical Command, U.S. Army

Peter Stuebe
Hazmat Operations, New York City Fire Department

Bruce Teele
National Fire Protection Association

Gary Tokle
National Fire Protection Association

James Tolson
Fairfax County Fire & Rescue, Local 2068

Edward Tomaszewski
Hazmat Operations, New York City Fire Department

Albert Turi
New York City Fire Department

Robert B. Walton
U.S. Air Force

Robert Weber
3M Company

Robert Weiderhold
U.S. Federal Bureau of Investigation

Andrew White
International Association of Fire Chiefs

William Williams
Hazmat, Oklahoma City Fire Department

Chief Enoch H. Williams, III
Defense Protective Service, U.S. Department of Defense

Charles Wood
U.S. Capitol Police

Hugh Wood
National Fire Programs, U.S. Federal Emergency Management Agency

Jim Zarzycki
Edgewood Chemical Biological Center, Army Soldier, Biological, Chemical Command, U.S. Army

Ralph Zumwalde
National Institute for Occupational Safety and Health, U.S. Centers for Disease Control and Prevention

RAND SCIENCE AND TECHNOLOGY POLICY INSTITUTE

David Adamson

James T. Bartis

Irene Brahmakulam

Scott Hassell

Ari Houser

Brian A. Jackson

Tom LaTourrette

D. J. Peterson

Jerry Sollinger

Ralda Williams

FACILITATORS (MARK KERBACK AND COMPANY, INC.)

Stephanie Becker

Betsy Bernstein

Lynn Greenberg

Mark Kerback

Janet Larson

Joseph Oliver

Jim Rubin

Eva Schmatz

Toni Sonet

Mary Stone

Appendix C

CONFERENCE AGENDA

NIOSH/RAND PERSONAL PROTECTIVE TECHNOLOGY CONFERENCE
DECEMBER 9–11, 2001
NEW YORK CITY

Sunday, December 9

6:00 – 7:00 pm	Reception hosted by International Safety Equipment Association

Monday, December 10

8:30 – 9:00	**Welcome**
	James T. Bartis, RAND Science and Technology Policy Institute
	Daniel Nigro, Chief, New York City Fire Department
	Kathleen M. Rest, Director, National Institute for Occupational Safety and Health
	Richard Metzler, Director, National Personal Protective Technology Laboratory
9:00 – 9:45	**Plenary Session 1**
	"Protecting America's Emergency Responders: The Government's Role in Domestic Defense" Richard Duffy *International Association of Fire Fighters*
	"Terrorism Response: The FDNY Experience" Dr. David Prezant *New York City Fire Department*

9:45 – 10:15	**Break**
10:15 – 12:15	**Panel Session 1 (8 concurrent meetings)**
12:15 – 1:15	**Lunch**
1:30 – 2:30	**Plenary Session 2**
	"Firefighters in a Changing World" Chief John Eversole (ret.) *International Association of Fire Chiefs*
	"Injuries and Illnesses Sustained by First Responders" Dr. Sandra Berrios-Torres *National Center for Injury Prevention and Control* Kara Perritt *National Institute for Occupational Safety and Health*
	"Protecting Workers at the World Trade Center Site" Don Carson *International Union of Operating Engineers*
2:30 – 5:00	**Panel Session 2 (8 concurrent meetings)**

Tuesday, December 11

8:00 – 9:00	**Plenary Session 3**
	"Lessons Learned from the Oklahoma City Response" Chief Sam Gonzales (ret.) *Federal Bureau of Investigation and Oklahoma City Police Department*
	"Lessons Learned from the Pentagon Response" Deputy Chief Enoch Williams, III *Defense Protective Service*
9:00 – 10:30	**Panel Session 3 (8 concurrent meetings)**
10:30 – 12:30	**Closing Plenary Session**
	Summaries of Panel Recommendations

SUMMARIES OF PLENARY PRESENTATIONS

Richard Duffy, International Association of Fire Fighters

"Protecting America's Emergency Responders: The Government's Role in Domestic Defense"

Mr. Duffy offered an overview of concerns related to domestic defense and a brief background of the International Association of Fire Fighters. He explained the Line of Duty Death Program, standard-setting by the National Fire Protection Association, and the role of the emergency responder. The presentation's main message was that firefighters' PPE initially meets standards and specifications, but it is unclear whether it continues to do so over time due to wear and maintenance. The talk concluded with two points: (1) The National Personal Protective Technology Laboratory needs to certify all protective equipment, not just respirators; and (2) firefighters need more protection and more confidence in the protective capability of their turnout clothing.

David Prezant, New York City Fire Department

"Terrorism Response: The FDNY Experience"

Dr. Prezant described a model for studying emergency response events and responder health outcomes, and a process for feeding these data back into PPE design. Health data from previous events led to improvements in PPE for firefighters in New York City, which in turn reduced burn injuries. However, firefighters using the new equipment experienced increased heat exhaustion. Dr. Prezant concluded that more protection is not necessarily better. Any analysis of World Trade Center responder health and injury outcomes needs to balance several considerations: protection for first responders versus worker comfort; ergonomic and fitness levels; and worker rotation to reduce exhaustion.

John Eversole, International Association of Fire Chiefs
"Firefighters in a Changing World"

John Eversole contended that the emergency-response world was not reinvented on September 11, 2001. Nuclear-biological-chemical response training programs already exist. The gas attack in Tokyo was cited as an example of an earlier event that improved preparedness. September 11 did show, however, that emergency responders are still not fully prepared to respond to large-scale acts of terrorism. It is time to get ahead of the curve in PPE, he argued. Specific examples of improvements in breathing apparatus were given. The talk emphasized the importance of certifying components as well as whole systems, which would promote interchangeability of parts and improve equipment availability.

Sandra Berrios-Torres, National Center for Injury Prevention and Control
Kara Perritt, National Institute for Occupational Safety and Health
"Injuries and Illnesses Sustained by First Responders"

The presentations focused on health care data and data issues related to the Oklahoma City and World Trade Center attacks. By October 14, more than 7,000 individuals had visited various treatment sites for health concerns related to the World Trade Center events. Specific data on the severity of these injuries were difficult to gather, however. The lack of perimeter control at the World Trade Center site made it difficult to monitor the extent of injury and illness. In effect, the "denominator" is unknown, as it was impossible to track how many people were at the site or measure their levels of exposure. It may be years before the true health effects of the disaster are known.

Don Carson, International Union of Operating Engineers
"Protecting Workers at the World Trade Center Site"

Mr. Carson characterized the World Trade Center as a heavy construction site. Construction workers' experiences at this site raised several concerns. Early on, it became clear that construction crews were wearing the wrong respirators and filters. Furthermore, fit-testing for respiratory equipment seldom occurred. Workers were not consistently informed of respiratory hazards, including freon and benzene. Employers are responsible for ensuring that the crews wear the proper PPE. Stressing the need for promoting greater awareness of hazards present on-site, Mr. Carson also emphasized the need for special training for construction workers participating in large-scale rescue and recovery operations.

Sam Gonzales, FBI and Oklahoma City Police Department
"Lessons Learned from the Oklahoma City Response"

The main lesson from Oklahoma City, Mr. Gonzales said, related to the importance of perimeter control. Until a scene is under control, no one can enforce rules for PPE. An issue related to site control is precertification and credentialing of health care personnel. He added that a critical, often overlooked concern from these types of incidents is mental health: Everyone involved is affected. Authorities need to do a better job of recognizing and meeting the need for mental-health care among all site personnel.

Enoch Williams, III, Defense Protective Service
"Lessons Learned from the Pentagon Response"

Mr. Williams stressed the importance of access and perimeter control. Perimeter control was established early at the Pentagon, but because of the sensitive nature of materials at the Pentagon, recovery was complicated. Planning and war-gaming exercises, as well as local coordination, are the keys to a well-executed emergency response. Players need to understand the command-and-control system, site workers need to have proper identification and credentials, and rules for PPE use need to be enforced.